About the author

The author at home working on his next book

Kevin Wraight is an historian with a keen interest for naval warfare. His first two books are *War at Sea* and *Battlefleet and Empire — A Brief History of the Royal Navy 1588 to 1922.* Alongside a successful career in business Kevin has been studying military history for over thirty years and his enthusiasm for the subject knows no bounds. In his own words Kevin wishes to "pass on my enthusiasm to the readers of my books and I hope they are both informed and entertained." Kevin was born in North London in 1971 and now resides in Devon.

WAR AT SEA
TWELVE NAVAL BATTLES THAT SHAPED THE WORLD

KEVIN WRAIGHT

WAR AT SEA
TWELVE NAVAL BATTLES THAT SHAPED THE WORLD

Vanguard Press

VANGUARD PAPERBACK

© Copyright 2021
Kevin Wraight

The right of Kevin Wraight to be identified as author of
this work has been asserted by him in accordance with the
Copyright, Designs and Patents Act 1988.

All Rights Reserved

No reproduction, copy or transmission of this publication
may be made without written permission.
No paragraph of this publication may be reproduced,
copied or transmitted save with the written permission of the
publisher, or in accordance with the provisions
of the Copyright Act 1956 (as amended).

Any person who commits any unauthorised act in relation to
this publication may be liable to criminal
prosecution and civil claims for damages.

A CIP catalogue record for this title is
available from the British Library.

ISBN 978 1 80016 163 4

*Vanguard Press is an imprint of
Pegasus Elliot MacKenzie Publishers Ltd.*
www.pegasuspublishers.com

First Published in 2021

**Vanguard Press
Sheraton House Castle Park
Cambridge England**

Printed & Bound in Great Britain

Dedication

In gratitude to all people of the sea, the only true enemy.

Contents

Introduction 11

Salamis 480 BC 13

Lepanto 1571 25

The Spanish Armada 1588 34

The Capture of Gibraltar 1704 45

Quiberon Bay 1759 55

The Saintes 1782 63

Trafalgar 1805 78

Tsushima 1905 89

Jutland 1916 101

Norway 1940 121

Midway 1942 130

The Falklands 1982 146

Epilogue 171

Introduction

From the first recorded battle at sea which historians believe to be 1210 BC when Suppiluliuma II, King of the Hittites, defeated a fleet from Cyprus and burned their ships, man has fought at sea. The purpose of this book is to show the influence of maritime warfare on history which has proven to be just as significant as warfare on land.

The twentieth century has seen some of the bitterest fighting and wars in the history of the world. We have seen new weapons and devastating ways of killing on land and in the air but at sea the strategies and tactics of over three thousand years still prevail as do the chief objectives of naval power. What are those objectives? To command the oceans and deny the enemy the freedom to use them. To control commerce and project influence and above all to allow freedom of movement of one's own forces and to assist in delivering armies onto hostile shores or prevent landing on home shores. On top of this command of the sea gives one the ability to strike where and when one chooses wrongfooting the enemy at every step. Of course not every battle at sea incorporates all these intentions, some will contain most if not all of them, others none at all but in history there were twelve sea battles that in my mind stand out for displaying all these objectives. This is not of course to demote other naval battles of history to secondary roles not as important as the twelve I have highlighted in this book. The battles between Rome and Carthage were of huge importance to the outcome of the Punic Wars as were the great battles of the age of sail. And of course how can we forget the part played by warships in the Normandy landings of Operation Overlord in 1944 and their part in winning the Pacific back from Japan in World War II. All these are examples of sea power as a defining part of history but I have to draw the line somewhere and this is why I have decided on the twelve battles of this narrative, each of which draw a direct line to significantly shaping the course of world history.

Salamis 480 BC

To tell the story of this pivotal ancient maritime battle of the Second Persian Invasion of Greece we must first go back to the First Persian Invasion of 492 – 490 BC. The vast and wealthy Persian Empire of this period was prominent in the middle east and keen to expand further west into Europe, Greece was seen as the gateway to this expansion by Darius the King of Persia. Greece at this time was made up of city-states all autonomous and self-governing rather than a collective nation. Most prominent of the city-states were Athens, Sparta and Eretria and Darius knew that he would have to reckon with these states if a conquest of Greece was to be successful.

Darius's own ambitions were given fuel by the recent revolt of cities in Ionia which had been brutally crushed by the Persians but created much anger and resentment towards Athens and Eretria who had openly supported the revolt. Darius was now committed to a full maritime invasion of Greece with the intention of subjugating all the city-states. In 492 BC his fleet transporting his army set sail for Greece landing first on the island of Naxos which the Persians sacked before moving on to subjugate Thrace and Macedon. However, the campaign ground to a halt there as the Persian fleet was lost at sea off Mount Athos. Darius then sent emissaries to all the Greek city-states demanding submission which was agreed to by all except Athens and Sparta. This led to the second campaign when Darius again set sail with a fleet to conquer most of the

Cycladic Islands landing finally at Eretria which after a short siege was captured, raised and the people taken as slaves. The fleet and army again set sail and landed at Marathon to move on Athens, the real prize.

The Athenian Army under Militades met the Persians at the Battle of Marathon sometime in August 490 BC and soundly defeated them causing heavy Persian losses for very few of their own. Indeed the father of history, Herodotus claimed that for two hundred and three Greek dead there were six thousand four hundred Persians killed. These figures have since been revised upwards and downwards respectively by modern historians but it still remains a significant Greek victory and one that would have a huge impact on the future of the Persian wars.

We come now to the second Persian invasion ten year later and the eventual battle of Salamis. Darius had always planned a further invasion of Greece but died in the intervening years leaving his son Xerxes to carry on his wishes. Did the Greeks know they would be back? Certainly, the great philosopher and prominent Athenian Themistocles was sure they would be back and when they came it would be by sea.

History remembers Themistocles as a philosopher and a proponent of democracy but he was also a strategic master who understood warfare, especially naval warfare and its importance. Themistocles was a populist, not an aristocrat. Athens at this time was a fledgling democracy which allowed the right people to rise to the top posts of government and Themistocles was one such citizen. He was elected Archon (ruler) in 493 BC and at once began building up the Athenian fleet to both meet the growing Persian threat and to protect the trade through the Black Sea which supplied Athens with most of its grain. Using his considerable oratory skills he convinced the Athenians to both build a fleet of two hundred triremes using the wealth generated from the recently located vein of silver at Laurium and move the fleet base from Phaleum to Piraeus, a much larger natural harbour which was easily defendable. There were also political implications to the raising of such a fleet, implications that highlight the democratic changes taking place in Athens at this time. The vast majority of the rowers were of the Athenian lower classes but being rowers in the navy that was to protect Athens and Greece pushed the lower orders up by making their voices heard, thus contributing to the development of democracy.

The trireme was the most complex and advanced warship of its time. Primarily a battering ram the trireme with its three rows of oars could cruise at six knots with a ramming speed of over eight knots. The Athenians became masters of the tactic of ramming and this was to prove decisive at the Battle of Salamis. The crew consisted of one hundred and seventy rowers, about ten deckhands for masts, steerage, maintenance etc and ten to twenty marines, usually fourteen Hoplites (citizen soldiers) and four archers.

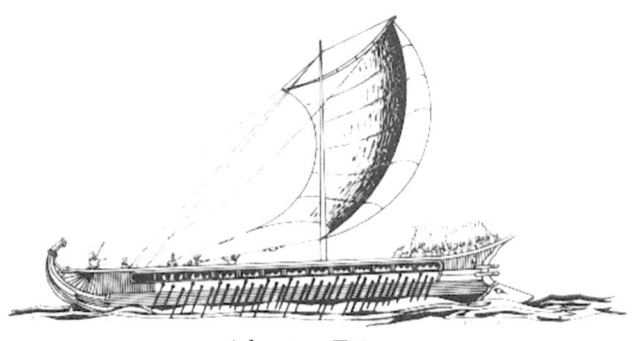

Athenian Trireme

As the Persian invasion of 480 BC became imminent and as was the practice of the time, the athenian's consulted the Oracle of Delphi who proclaimed that *'Only a wall of wood would stand intact against the enemy'*. This led to serious debate among the Athenians who were split between thinking it meant either a palisade or a navy. Themistocles interpreted this as meaning the navy and considered this to be confirmed by a later Oracle prediction that *'Blessed Salamis, you will be the death of mothers' sons'*. Again, using his oratory skills, he convinced Athens that the navy was the key to victory in the forthcoming war. The invasion when it came was vast. Estimates put the Persian Army at over two hundred thousand strong with a fleet of over thirteen hundred ships in support. A huge pontoon bridge was erected over the Hellespont (Dardanelles) spanning three miles in length, an extraordinary achievement for its time alongside that of a canal built across the Mount Athos peninsular to avoid a recurrence of the loss of the fleet which had occurred in the first invasion.

Greece and the Aegean

Faced with invasion yet again a small number of Greek city-states had agreed to put aside their differences and form a loose alliance for the defence of Greece. They elected the Spartans to lead them in overall command of the armies and navies and set up two lines of defence, one at Thermopylae and Artemisium and the second at the narrow isthmus to the Peloponnese west of Athens. Initially, a small force of Spartans under their King Leonidas heroically held the narrow pass of Thermopylae for three crucial days being finally overwhelmed after a traitor showed the Persians a path around the pass that led to an attack in the rear of the Spartans. At the same time, the Greek Navy consisting of predominantly Athenian ships under the command of Themistocles engaged the Persian supporting fleet at Artemisium. After an indecisive battle lasting several days, the Greek fleet withdrew to Salamis having been unable to make a dent in the huge Persian fleet. There was nothing now in the way of the Persian Army and Athens was plundered after the navy had evacuated most of the citizens to the island of Salamis and the army withdrew to the neck of land connecting the mainland of Greece to the Peloponnese. Here a wall was built which would hold the Persians for a time but the Persian Navy could easily land troops behind the wall, the Persian Navy had to be dealt with. Themistocles realised he could not defend the entire coastline so he had to bring about a decisive battle and the best place to engage the Persians was off Salamis. The tides and currents were perfect and in the Greek's favour and the Persian numerical superiority could be offset by their inability to deploy all at once in the narrow seas.

What happened next is a matter of historical debate to this day but what is certain is that Themistocles sent an emissary to Xerxes with the intention of pretending to defect. His message to Xerxes was that the Greek alliance was falling apart and that the remaining Greek states were wanting to withdraw from Salamis back to the Peloponnese and that Xerxes should bring his fleet in to stop them. The approach by Themistocles to

Xerxes was certainly made and definitely in character for Themistocles who was clever, but it is unknown if the other Greeks were a party to this deception. One version of events is that Themistocles, fearing the Greek allies would withdraw, engineered the Persian intervention. I do not know but would hazard a guess that there was collusion as the Athenian Navy would need the assistance of the remaining Greek navies to confront Xerxes in battle. There is also the religious aspect, most Greeks would have believed the Oracle of Delphi and put their faith in its prophesies, this combined with Themistocles's persuasive oratory could well have convinced them of this plan. In addition to this despite the wall at the neck of the corridor to the Peloponnese the Persians could very likely not be stopped so another way had to be found. We will never know for sure.

The following morning after patrolling all night outside the entrance to the Straits of Salamis Xerxes appears to have lost patience and expecting a crushing victory ordered his fleet in to attack the Greek Navy. There were cooler heads present including Queen Artemisia of Halicarnassus who tried to persuade Xerxes not to fight as there was no need but they did not prevail.

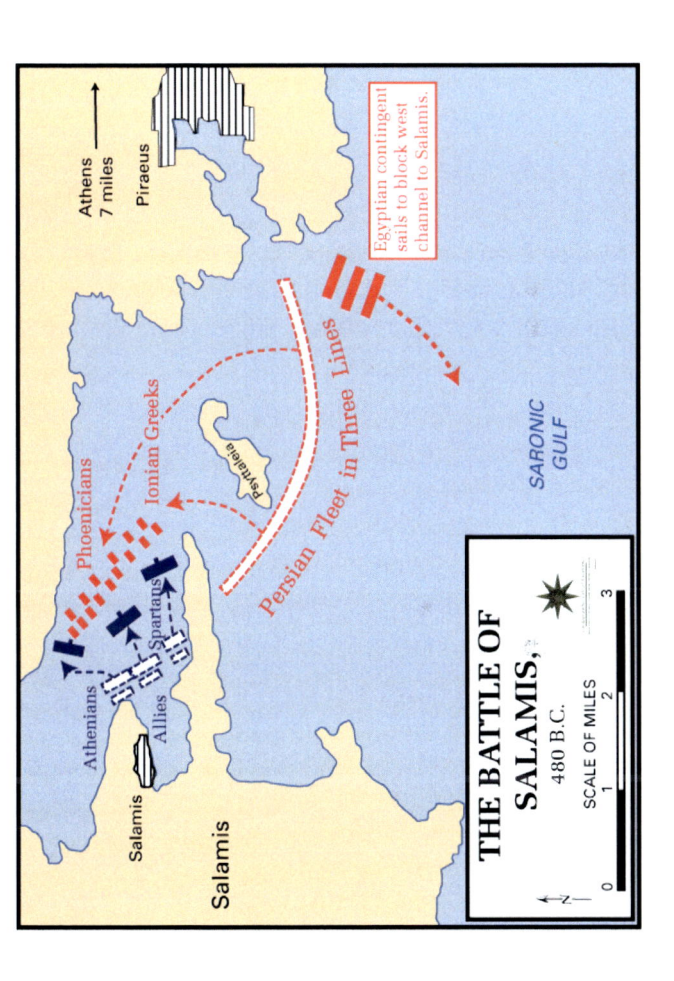

The Battle of Salamis has not been covered in depth by writings at the time so the best we can do is surmise events based on known tactics, currents, tides etc and the recorded losses, but as far as historians can make out the battle very likely played out as follows. Xerxes ordered his fleet to sail into the Straits of Salamis at dawn whilst at the same time landing a small contingent of four hundred men on the island of Pysttaleia in order to capture any Greeks who might swim ashore in the forthcoming battle. The Greek Navy appears to have lined up in the straits probably from north to south. It has been suggested that they lined up from east to west but I think this unlikely as it would have meant their left flank being off a hostile coast. A small force of Corinthian ships appears to have been sent north to cover the northern entrance to the straits in fear of Persian ships attempting a pincer movement but this does not appear to have happened and the ships returned later in the day to fight.

The Persian fleet entered the bay in much disorder and crammed together presenting a perfect target for the Greek Navy who attacked and slowly forced the Persian ships back on to the second and third waves approaching from the entrance. The tactics employed by both fleets would be to preferably ram and sink the enemy ship, if not sail up the side of the enemy ship, snap the oars and disable it, lastly boarding if necessary. The conditions for ramming would most certainly have been in the Greeks' favour with the Persian ships crammed together and unable to manoeuvre properly and this accounts for the heavy Persian losses.

At some stage in the battle, it began to fall apart for the Persians when Xerxes's brother Ariabignes commanding the right flank of the Persian fleet was killed and the right flank became even more disorganised withdrawing in on itself with many ships running aground. At this point according to Herodotus Queen Artemesia in command of a division of Persian ships started to flee the battle pursued by a Greek ship. In a clever though dishonourable ruse, she rammed a friendly Persian ship and attacked it in the hope that the pursuing Greek ship would break off the chase thinking she was engaged by a friendly Greek ship. It worked and Artemesia got away. This highlights quite clearly the disorganised battle taking place where in the heat of combat and because of all the different ship types and nationalities involved it became unclear exactly who was who. Even Xerxes watching from his throne atop a nearby mountain cheered when he saw Artemesia attacking the friendly ship believing it to be Greek. This led him to say, *'My men have become women and my women become men'*. By this stage it was practically all over and the Persians had been driven back out of the straits eventually withdrawing to Phaleum. The final gruesome act was the Athenian General Aristides landing on the island of Pysttaleia and slaughtering the Persian garrison left there by Xerxes.

In the aftermath of the battle Xerxes retreated with most of his army back over the Hellespont fearing that the Greek Navy might destroy the pontoon bridge and cut him off. The war was not over however as he left part of his army under Mardonius to continue the campaign which ended in final defeat for the Persians at Platea in 479 BC.

I do not think that the Greek victory at Salamis can be overrated, so much was at stake for the future of the western world. Had the Persians been victorious Greece would have been subjugated and the democratic revolution started in Athens in 508 BC would have been stifled. Athens would not have reached its zenith as the great cradle of civilisation which has given us so much in the way of politics, philosophy, science, art and culture. It would have meant the future influence of the middle east into western Europe and perhaps with the coming of Islam in the 7th century a strong foothold of that religion and culture. An immediate aftermath of course was the beginning of the breakdown of the Persian conquests in Greece. Within thirty years Macedon, Thrace, the islands of the Aegean and finally Ionia would be free of Persia and more importantly future Greeks would have a foothold in Asia Minor, a foothold exploited by Alexander the Great.

Lepanto 1571

The victors of Lepanto
John of Austria, Marcantonio Colonna and Sebastiano Venier

This has to be one of the most interesting battles in history as it occurred at a time when the old medieval way of warfare was slowly giving way to the new age of gunpowder and sailing ships. Lepanto was the last great clash of galleys, that hugely important weapon which was so influential to the Mediterranean theatre of history. We see here the clash of two prominent world religions and cultures that would shape the western world much as Salamis did two thousand years before and in that same corner of eastern Europe that was such a hot spot for the clash of east versus west.

The battle took place during the Ottoman Venetian War of 1570 to 1573. A war that was purely one of conquest for the Ottomans and one of defence for the Venetian Republic. The initial target of Ottoman conquest was the strategically important island of Cyprus. This island stuck out into a region of Ottoman interest rather like a sea locked bulge. Very close to the mainland of Asia Minor and straddling the all-important trade routes from the Levant, Cyprus also had its own wealth from cotton and sugar. Cyprus was one of the most important and significant overseas possessions of the rich trading state of the Venetian Republic and had long been sought after by the Ottoman Empire.

In 1568 peace was concluded between the Ottoman Empire and the Kingdom of Hungary bringing an end to a long and protracted war that had proved costly for both sides. The advent of peace allowed the Sultan of the Ottoman Empire, Selim II, to turn his attention to Cyprus, a threat long anticipated by the Venetians who fearing an attack had poured resources into the defence of the island. Despite the reinforcements however the island was by no means secure and Selim calculated that a swift attack could capture the island from the Venetians before they could react. An invasion could also be made easier as the mainly Greek Orthodox population of Cyprus was not entirely happy with their Catholic overlords and in some cases would welcome an Ottoman take over, how they would fare in that event though was not clear as Islam at times could be equally intolerant of other religions.

In 1570 an ultimatum was sent to the Venetian Republic by Selim II demanding that Cyprus be ceded to the Ottoman Empire in exchange for more trading rights and lands in Dalmatia. The ultimatum was not dismissed without some consideration but eventually refused on the grounds that the Venetians believed that they could form a Catholic alliance against Ottoman aggression and perhaps see off an attack. The Ottomans finally invaded Cyprus at the end of June 1570. The Venetian fleet of about one hundred galleys withdrew unable to confront the vastly superior Ottoman fleet of around four hundred galleys allowing the landing of eighty thousand Ottoman troops. The Venetian defenders withdrew into the forts surrounding Nicosia but these and the city itself fell in early September with twenty thousand of Nicosia's inhabitants being massacred, the rest being taken as slaves. The Ottoman Army then went on to besiege Famagusta in early 1571, this city finally fell in August and the garrison was imprisoned, the commanders being executed. Events were already moving for the Venetians in the shape of the forming of a Holy League which had been proposed and put together on the instigation of Pope Pius V to come to the aid of Cyprus with a combined fleet of two hundred galleys and fifty thousand men under the command of John of Austria, an illegitimate son of Charles V the Holy Roman Emperor and half-brother of Philip II of Spain.

The combined fleet of mainly Venetian galleys with naval elements from Genoa, Spain, the Papal States and the orders of the Knights of Malta, St Lazarus and St Stephen set sail from Messina in August 1571 to relieve Famagusta arriving in late September at Corfu where news of the fall of Famagusta was received. Despite this set back the league was intent on battle as it would need to destroy the Ottoman fleet before it could land its fifty thousand troops on Cyprus. Equally the Ottoman fleet was keen to fight the allied fleet in order to remove any threat of the Allies re-taking Cyprus and equally as important clearing the Mediterranean of enemy ships to secure further expansion west.

On 7th October 1571, the allied fleet of two hundred and six galleys and six galleasses arrived in the Gulf of Petras to confront the Ottoman fleet. Both sides employed galleys as the main weapons of naval combat. Partly powered by sail and partly by oars the galley had changed little from the triremes of ancient times but the tactics were now slightly different in that it was more common to try and take enemy galleys by boarding rather than ramming, thus there was a higher proportion of soldiers than in ancient times. The galleys of the 16th century also carried artillery and this is where the Allies had an advantage as their fleet carried over twice as many guns as the Ottoman fleet.

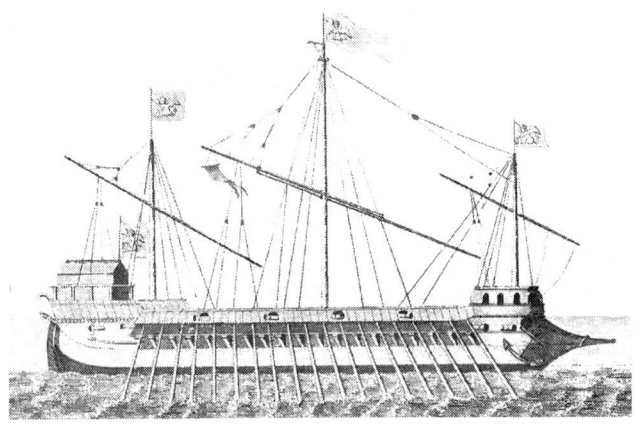

Galleass

The allied soldiers were also armed with muskets and hand guns whereas the Ottomans still used the composite bow. As I stated earlier this really was a clash of the old and the new. Both sides had vast amounts of oarsmen to power their galleys but there were subtle differences. The Venetian fleet (about half of the allied fleet) had freemen as oarsmen, the rest of the allied fleet used slaves and convicts but released them from their chains before the battle. The Ottoman oarsmen were all slaves, mainly Christian and this would have an impact on the battle as we shall see.

On seeing the Ottoman fleet John of Austria decided to attack straight away fearing that his loose coalition would fall apart and deployed his force into four divisions: The left (northern) of fifty-five galleys, the centre of sixty-four galleys, the right of fifty-five galleys with a reserve behind the centre of thirty-eight galleys. The Ottoman fleet was similarly arrayed with a right (northern) division of sixty-two assorted galleys of different sizes, a centre of 64 assorted galleys and the left of ninety-three assorted galleys with a reserve behind the centre of ninety-six assorted galleys. Battle commenced with the long-range fire of the allied galleasses causing damage and confusion to the approaching Ottoman fleet when at around noon the allied left clashed with the Ottoman right. Despite being as close to the southern shore as possible the Allies could not prevent a few Ottoman ships from flanking them and the clash of the two northern divisions soon developed into violent hand to hand to fighting. It was said that a man could walk from ship to ship they were that close together. The tide was soon turning in the Allies favour with the release of Christian slaves from the Ottoman galleys who took up arms and fought back at their previous captors.

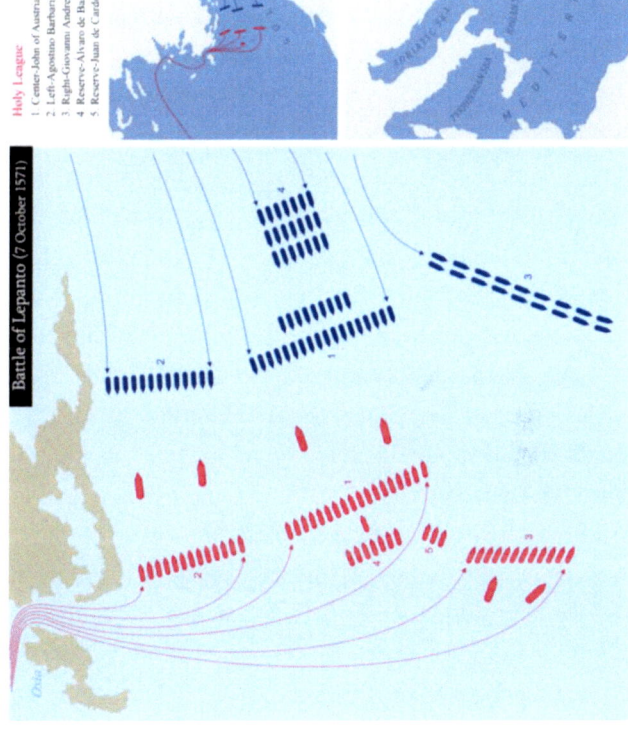

Meanwhile the centre divisions had come together and much hard fighting saw this part of the battle very much in the balance. The fighting soon centred around the clash of the opposing flagships with what was very likely to be the imminent fall of the allied flagship which was locked together in combat with the flagship of Ali Pasha the Ottoman Admiral. To the south the right-wing division of the allied fleet had swung too far out to the south on the orders of its commander who mistakenly thought that the Ottomans were trying to out-flank him. This opened a gap which the Ottoman left wing exploited by moving in and attacking the allied centre from the flank. Events soon swung back in the Allies' favour however with the deployment of the reserve to counter the Ottomans' flank attack. The pressure on the allied flagship was reduced when an allied galley came alongside the allied flagship and helped capture the Ottoman flagship killing Ali Pasha in the process. The Holy League banner was quickly raised on the enemy flagship and seeing that the admiral was either dead or captured the Ottoman fleet began to lose heart and fall apart. The battle was over by early evening culminating in an historic and significant allied victory. The Ottoman fleet had lost one hundred and eighty-seven galleys taken or destroyed along with forty thousand prisoners and dead, the Allies suffering around seven thousand five hundred casualties.

Despite this victory of the Holy League at Lepanto the Ottomans still came out on top in the peace of 1573.

The Venetian Republic was not able to recover Cyprus and had to cede it to the Ottoman Empire along with an indemnity of three hundred thousand ducats as part of the peace terms. However even though the real victory of Lepanto may not have been realised the future was set by the success of the allied fleet. Ottoman dominance of the Mediterranean theatre was stopped in its tracks by Lepanto and a clear demarcation was drawn with the Ottomans being confined to the eastern Mediterranean leaving the western nations free to develop under Christianity and the renaissance. Victory gave the nations of the western Mediterranean a confidence in facing up to the Ottoman Empire which ultimately led to the empire's downfall through its failure to expand further west.

The Spanish Armada 1588

Queen Elizabeth I

Toward the end of the 16th century, we see great mariners such as Drake, Hawkins, Raleigh and Frobisher sailing the seas of the world promoting English power, raiding Spanish shipping (which was a huge boost to the English economy), founding new lands such as Virginia in the Americas and most importantly honing the skills of seamanship which were to prove so vital in the centuries to come. England's mariners were to come into contact with Spain many times during the latter half of the 16th century. There were numerous attacks on Spanish shipping and colonies which coupled with the Protestant religion in England was to lead inevitably to open conflict with Spain.

Spain of course had set herself up as the protector of the Catholic Church and took a keen interest in the plight of Catholics in England. Elizabeth was all for free religious practices, however all the plots against her appear to have been Catholic in origin when uncovered by Elizabeth's master spy Francis Walsingham. There was also at this time a great drive within England to convert intellectuals to Catholicism and the religion was going from strength to strength. In the eyes of Philip II the internal English religious dispute was brought to a head with the execution of Mary Queen of Scots after it was proved she was openly plotting to usurp the throne of England. Mary had rather foolishly and naively been involved in a plot constructed by Walsingham and involving the merchant, Anthony Babington. This act coupled with the practice of Catholicism eventually being made illegal in England was all the religious ammunition Phillip needed to justify war with Elizabeth's England.

Philip saw this war as a crusade and openly sought the support of Pope Sixtus V but the pope set certain conditions on his support. These were to have a dramatic effect on the success of the armada and can even provide the reason for the failure. Spain's other concerns were the blatant attacks on her shipping by English gentlemen mariners and privateers. These were made worse by the fact that the queen openly encouraged the attacks and indeed profited by them both personally and for the nation. At this time England was also openly assisting the Protestant Dutch in their fight against Catholic Spain, so a formal clash of arms was inevitable. Thus, Philip II of Spain finally decided in 1586 to embark on the 'enterprise of England'.

In 1586 Philip turned to the Marquis of Santa Cruz, his most able military strategist, and instructed him to form a plan for the invasion of England. Santa Cruz's plan was perfect in its conception and had this been the plan that was followed would most likely have succeeded. Santa Cruz decided that an army of fifty-five thousand soldiers transported by a fleet of eighty thousand tons and escorted by six galleasses, forty galleys and two hundred landing craft should sail to South East England and land in Kent as a prelude to an attack on London.

However, this plan could not be followed due to the conditions set by Pope Sixtus V. He was not willing to make this a political or national gain by Spain and certainly not an attempt to extend the empire. Therefore, his condition was that the army employed must be led by the Duke of Parma, an Italian (albeit nephew of Philip II). This changed the strategy completely and meant that a compromise of the Santa Cruz plan was required. This revised plan was that the fleet would have to sail to the Low Countries, rendezvous with and embark Parma's army, then carry out a landing on the south coast of England. Santa Cruz was furious at this revised plan and quite rightly pointed out the flaws and dangers connected with it. His main concerns were that the fleet would have to sail up channel and then attempt to meet with an army (already engaged) and embark it in Dutch waters where the Dutch Navy was well versed in fighting, all this whilst fighting off the English Navy. Philip's mind however was made up, this was the plan engaged and thus were sown the seeds of failure.

The building up of the armada began in earnest with the requisitioning and building of ships. This of course takes time and the attrition suffered by the armada was a constant drain on its resources, a situation not helped by Drake's pre-emptive strike on Cadiz in 1587 which destroyed much materiel and caused the expedition to be put back a year. In January 1588 Santa Cruz, worn out by his service died. Philip chose as his successor the Duke of Medina Sidonia, Spain's foremost nobleman and an able military commander.

The English fleet assembled on the south coast to meet this threat was quite a bit different to the Spanish fleet. It must be remembered that the English had been used to attacking Spanish vessels for some time whereas the Spanish ships and crews were more used to convoy escort. This gave the English a distinct edge which was increased by the use of a remarkable English ship

Prince Philip II of Spain

design, the race-built galleon. Far different to the large battleships built by Henry VIII these ships were built for speed and for the use of heavy artillery. The race-built galleon was so named from the term *raised* to denote the raised fore and aft castles.

Ironically the preparedness of the English fleet was very much down to the organisational skills of Philip himself. He was after all King of England from 1554 to 1558 whilst married to Queen Mary. Whilst in this position he administered the English Navy and turned it around from the sorry bankrupt state it was left in by Henry. Also, at this crucial time the Navy Board was headed by that great seafarer John Hawkins. He was instrumental in preparing the navy for the coming fight and built the first ever dry dock at Deptford on the Medway. The English also possessed the best canon at this time, they were iron rather than bronze and although bronze was widely recognised to be superior to iron it was much more expensive. However English iron ore possessed certain mineral properties which rendered the iron far stronger and more flexible than iron from other regions, thus making the canon almost as good as the bronze pieces but much cheaper and easier to produce.

On 28th May 1588, the fleet sailed from Lisbon arriving off Ushant in late July. It then began its run up the channel arrayed in a crescent formation with divisions to the left and right ready to sally out and engage any enemy that presented itself.

The English Admiral Lord Howard of Effingham had sought the advice of Francis Drake over fleet deployment and Drake advised that the fleet station itself in Plymouth, for two reasons, mainly:

1. It can protect the West Country which could be a potential landing zone.
2. More importantly, it gave the English the weather gauge, essential in any battle at this time, especially with the prevailing south westerly winds.

The armada sailed slowly up channel and the English fleet slipped in neatly behind it. There then began the bombardment of the Spanish ships by the English with ships individually sailing forth, firing and then returning to formation. The Spanish flank guards could not intercept these as it meant sailing into the wind, so the Spanish fleet had to endure this punishment. However, the bombardment was not particularly successful and the English were quite rightly concerned about how to stop this vast fleet. It was Drake who provided the first major victory of the ongoing sea fight when he captured the *Nuestra Seniora Del Rosario*. Admittedly he was after treasure and had indeed disobeyed orders but it was an important victory all the same in that it provided intelligence on the handling of the guns in Spanish ships and showed that it could take up to a day to reload.

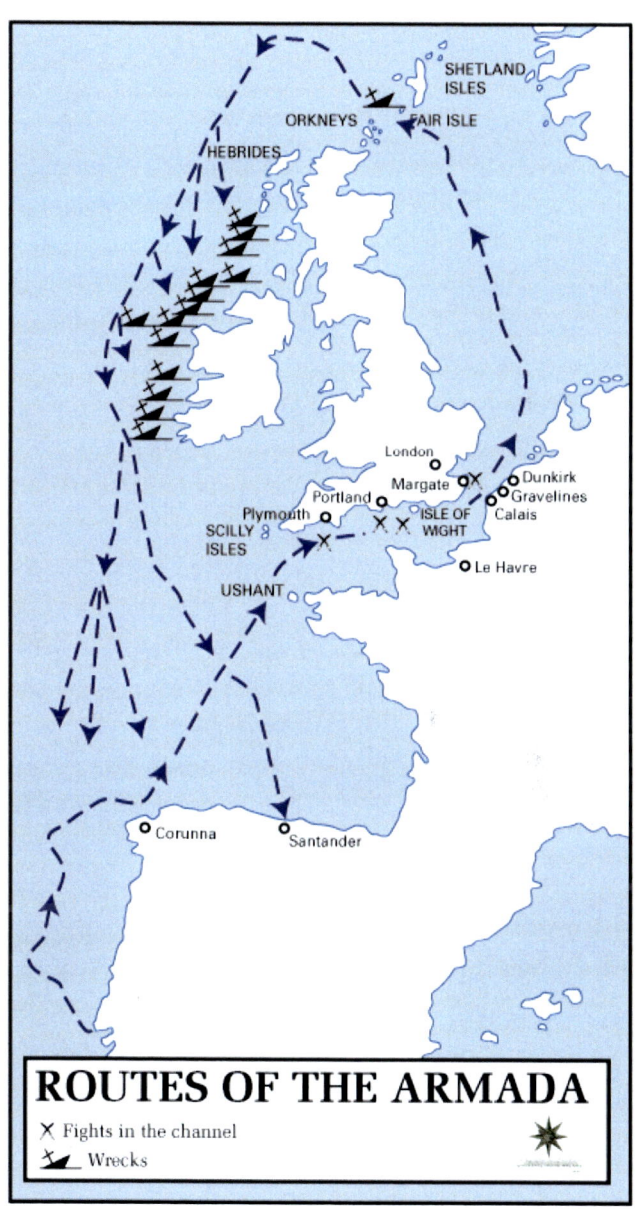

The Spanish fleet were uncertain of the location of Parma's army anchored off Calais and sent riders to find Parma. This presented the English with the perfect opportunity to use fire ships which they sent in under cover of darkness with a strong prevailing wind. The resultant chaos and panic inflicted on the Spanish caused most of the armada to cut its moorings and scatter. Medina Sidonia and the bulk of the fighting ships regrouped the scattered fleet and moved further up the coast into Dutch waters pursued by the English still bombarding them.

At this critical stage the armada found itself off Gravelines where they were engaged again in earnest by the English. Many Spanish ships were damaged and a few were sunk or run aground, however the effect on Spanish moral was hugely deleterious. Had the armada been the self-contained force that Santa Cruz had insisted on then it could have landed the army in southern England without any opposition. However, the armada found itself off a hostile coast and no army in sight. Medina Sidonia realised he could not remain where he was for fear of more fire ships so in the absence of Parma, he had no choice but to keep moving. This meant inevitably north and into the gales of the North Sea. The English (out of ammunition) pursued the Spanish fleet as far as the coast of lowland Scotland where it broke off pursuit. As the armada made its way round Scotland and Ireland it lost ships on the hazardous coastlines of those countries until the tired and diseased crews finally found their way back to Spain.

The war with Spain provided vast amounts of money and treasure for the national economy but more importantly it was a successful and moral boosting enterprise for English sailors and ships. Not only do we see the fight against the armada but also countless smaller actions involving the capture of Spanish treasure ships and the highly successful raid on Cádiz carried out by Drake in 1587. The destruction of the armada was to lead to bankruptcy for Spain on the death of the Spanish King Philip II in 1599 and this allowed England to supplant Spain as the world's leading naval power.

After the defeat of the armada English mariners were able to exploit the victory by sailing further into the south seas where they broke in to the lucrative Spanish and Portuguese trade with India and the Far East. This culminated with Raleigh's capture of the Portuguese galleon *Madre De Deus* in August 1592 and with it much treasure and wealth. Far more important though was the seizure of the ship's rutter or mariner's handbook. The rutter (a precursor to charts) contained sailing directions and navigation information of the trade routes to the countries of the Far East such as Japan and China.

On 31st December 1600, the East India Company was officially formed with the intention of sending trade ships to the Far East which it did every year for the next sixteen years. The company also established trading posts ashore in India in 1612 and Japan in 1613. These laid the foundations for one of the most successful and richest trade companies of the age and began the road to empire for Britain. The East India Company would come to dominate India entirely with its private army and navy and provide one of the wealthiest sources of trade for the British Empire.

Therefore, when we consider the episode of the armada we should not perhaps think only in terms of the long tenacious channel fight and the subsequent destruction of the Spanish fleet but also of the effect on the history of the world as a consequence. The failure of the armada is for me one of the pivotal maritime moments which has shaped the world. It could be argued that without the defeat of the armada and subsequent bankruptcy of Spain, England may not actually have emerged as the world power she became. The war with Spain saw the decline of one empire and the rise of another, a pattern constantly repeated in history

The Capture of Gibraltar 1704

George Rooke

In early November 1700 the Spanish King Charles II died childless leaving the two great royal houses of western Europe, the French Bourbons and Austrian Habsburgs to squabble over the throne. This would lead to the War of the Spanish Succession which waged from 1701 to 1714 and encompassed most of the globe. Although Charles II of Spain had bequeathed the throne to his great nephew Philip, Philip was grandson to the king of France, Louis XIV and the rest of Europe was very uneasy at France and Spain potentially combining as one, especially as Philip was also a potential heir to Louis XIV. This was the most prominent cause of the war but there were also territorial and trade disputes which helped to oil the wheels and when war broke out France faced a Grand Alliance of Britain, The Holy Roman Empire, The Netherlands and Habsburg Spain, later joined by Prussia and Portugal, the purpose of the alliance was to put the Habsburg candidate the Archduke Charles (Charles III of Spain), son of Leopold I of The Holy Roman Empire on the throne of Spain.

The land campaigns of John Churchill Duke of Marlborough are of course well documented but I wish here to concentrate on one of the major naval enterprises of the war. The capture of Gibraltar was almost an accident with very little consequence at the time but it is a pivotal part in the history of western Europe and the Mediterranean and a cornerstone of the building of the British Empire.

At the start of the war the Allies were keen to gain a foothold and port on the Iberian peninsula and sights were set on Cadiz for this purpose. This would allow a fleet to operate in the western Mediterranean and bottle up the French fleet at Toulon preventing it from joining the French fleet at Brest. In September 1702 an Anglo-Dutch fleet set sail for Cadiz with the intention of laying siege and capturing the port. However, the defences proved too strong and the allied fleet under Admiral George Rooke and the Dutch Admiral Van Almonde were forced to withdraw. Luck was with Rooke though as on the 23rd October 1702 whilst withdrawing from Cadiz the allied fleet encountered the rich Spanish treasure fleet returning from the Americas. In a decisive action known as the Battle of Vigo Bay the allied fleet of fifteen sail of the line completely destroyed the Franco-Spanish fleet of fifteen sail of the line three galleons and seventeen galleys without loss. This was a significant victory and turned the tables very much in the Allies favour who were now dominant in the region. The victory also convinced the Portuguese King Peter II to sever his ties with the Bourbons and join the Grand Alliance in 1703. This gave the Allies the use of the port of Lisbon which would allow them to operate in the Mediterranean.

The allied fleet in 1704 now working jointly with Prince George of Hesse-Darmstadt was now in the Mediterranean with the intention of capturing what was thought to be the sympathetic port of Barcelona. Hesse was convinced that a show of force would encourage the Catalan people to rise up in defiance of Philip and champion their preferred candidate Archduke Charles whom they called Charles III. The Allies attempted to capture Barcelona in May 1704 but without success. The uprising did not occur, the defences of Barcelona were too strong and again the allied fleet was forced to retire. On top of this set back news reached Admiral Rooke that the French fleet under the Comte de Toulouse had left Brest and was attempting to join the fleet at Toulon. Rooke set sail to intercept but was unable to catch them. This temporarily gave the French fleet the initiative in numbers however Rooke was joined by a reinforcing fleet under Admiral Sir Cloudesley Shovell and this redressed the balance of power. The allied fleet moved south to anchor off the north African coast and a council of war was held at sea to decide what to do next. Things had not gone well and even though the fleet had gained a victory at Vigo Bay they had not carried out their main objective which was to achieve a foothold on the peninsular. Hesse argued for another attack on Cadiz but the naval party was against this fearing the defences were too strong. After a long discussion it was decided that Gibraltar could be taken and more importantly held with the forces at their command. It was not the foothold envisaged as the harbour was small and there was no trade coming through it but it was lightly defended and once in the allies' possession could provide a forward base of operations with Lisbon still being the main port.

Prince George of Hesse-Darmstadt

The fleet arrived off Gibraltar on 1st August 1704, and under covering fire from an inshore squadron of twenty-two ships under Admiral Byng Hesse landed on the isthmus to the north of Gibraltar town with eighteen hundred British and Dutch marines. Very weak resistance in the form of a small contingent of cavalry was soon brushed aside thus cutting off the isthmus from mainland Spain. Hesse then contacted the governor of Gibraltar Don Diego de la Salinas and asked for his surrender which was refused. Salinas, a brave man was not unaware of his predicament and though hopeful of relief from the mainland he was sure this would not come, however he would hold out as long as he could as a matter of honour. The garrison was tiny, only fifty-six regular troops and several hundred militia (who fled as soon as Byng's force came into sight) along with one hundred guns, most of which did not work and had no crews.

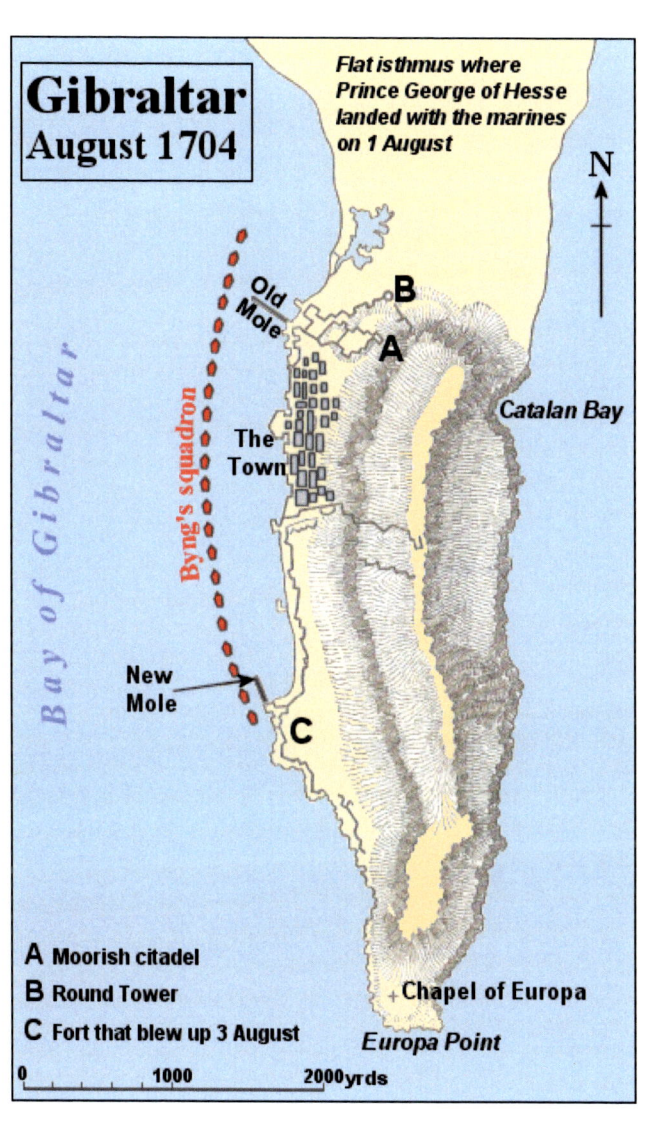

The failure of achieving a Spanish surrender led to a gradual turning of the screw starting early on the 3rd August with the eighty gun ship of the line *HMS Dorsetshire* attacking and capturing a French privateer which was tied up on the old mole and had been carrying out a steady fire on the marines to the north. This was followed by Byng's inshore squadron warping (being towed) closer to the town and beginning a huge bombardment. This was an earnest attempt to put pressure on the defenders as the French fleet under Toulouse was approaching from the north east so capture of the town was essential before they arrived. The next stage was a landing of several hundred seamen on the new mole to the south of the town. This was carried out easily as the defenders of the fort on the mole had departed, however tragedy occurred when the powder store exploded in an accident killing nearly two hundred seamen. The party then pushed north and captured the southern walls around the town hoisting the flag and after further reinforcements under Byng landed and joined the party the town was fully besieged from north and south. On 4th August Salinas surrendered.

The allied fleet had now to move out of the Straits of Gibraltar to confront the French fleet so leaving the marines to hold the town and the old Moorish fort Rooke moved the fleet east. The Battle of Malaga was not as decisive a battle as Vigo Bay, both the fleets engaged and much damage was done to each other but no ships lost, the French withdrawing back to Toulon. The Allies were unable to follow due to damage and lack of powder and shot from the bombardment of Gibraltar but in strategic terms this was a huge allied victory. A foothold had been gained on the peninsular and even though it was not as expected was still significant and with future potential. The Allies retained possession of Gibraltar until the end of the war when it was formerly ceded to Britain under the treaty of Utrecht. In my view this is where the capture of Gibraltar is so important. Had the original attacks on Cadiz or Barcelona succeeded it is unlikely that the Allies would have captured Gibraltar as there would be no need for it but on the ending of the war is it likely that Cadiz or Barcelona could have been retained by Britain unlike the small, seemingly unimportant town of Gibraltar? This to me is the real victory as I believe it most unlikely that Britain could have retained such key parts of Spain as Cadiz and Barcelona.

The War of the Spanish Succession ended in 1714 with Philip retaining the throne of Spain but relinquishing any claim to the French throne. As mentioned above Gibraltar would remain in British hands and would prove vital in the story of the British Empire right up to this day. Spain has tried several times to regain Gibraltar by diplomatic means without success. It is now a British overseas territory with a British population and will not be handed back to Spain.

I think that Spain's request is not unreasonable but one cannot but think of a degree of hypocrisy in their claim as they themselves hold overseas territories which they have no intention of relinquishing.

Quiberon Bay 1759

Edward Hawke

The Seven Years War has often been called the first true world war as it covered three continents and all the world's oceans and the Royal Navy was instrumental in Britain's military success, on the continent of North America especially. Britain's dominance in North America can be attributed to the army and land campaigns on a tactical basis but it was the Royal Navy who provided the strategic background for the victories on land by controlling the Atlantic Ocean and stopping the French from reinforcing their territories in New France. This strategic control was gained in 1759 with two of the most important battles in British history. These battles tend to be overlooked as Trafalgar has always been considered the biggest Royal Navy strategic victory in the age of sail but this chapter will show how the defeat of two French fleets would allow Britain to dominate the oceans and ultimately the new world and provide the ingredients for Britain's famous *'Annus Mirablis'* the year of wonder. The two battles are of course of Lagos and Quiberon Bay. I prefer to view these as part of the same overall picture and with this in mind I link them together for the purposes of this book and the reader will understand why as we progress through this narrative.

During 1759 the French devised a plan to invade England and Scotland by landing an army on the south coast and a follow up army in Scotland to incite rebellion against the Hanoverian monarchy. In order to achieve this an army was assembled near Vannes in Brittany and the French fleet at Toulon was ordered to sail to join the French fleet at Brest, link up and carry the army to England.

In May 1759 Admiral Boscawen was ordered to blockade Toulon whilst Admiral Sir Edward Hawke blockaded Brest. The First Sea Lord Admiral Anson had conceived the strategically inspired plan to sit the fleet to the NNW of Ushant. This allowed blockade of Brest (with an inshore squadron of frigates to observe and call in the main fleet in the event of a breakout) and to sit amid the trade routes back to England covering any incoming convoys.

In late July 1759 Boscawen was forced back to Gibraltar with his fleet of fourteen sail of the line arriving on 4th August to revictual and replace hands lost to action and disease. On 5th August the French fleet of twelve sail of the line under Admiral La Clue left Toulon headed for Cadiz and then the mouth of the Loire to collect the army assembled at Vannes. On 17th August the French fleet was spotted heading through the Straits of Gibraltar and Boscawen immediately gave chase in two divisions several hours apart. La Clue seeing this ordered his fleet to head out into the Atlantic for fear of being bottled up in Cadiz. However only half his fleet complied with this order, it is not known precisely why, either the following ships did not see the signal and the change in course in the diminishing daylight or the captains decided to continue to a friendly port. We know not which but bearing in mind there is always safety in numbers and with darkness fast approaching the chances of losing the British were high if the whole fleet continued out to sea together, I suspect it was the former reason of the two. In any event the next morning La Clue hove too to await the rest of his fleet and saw eight sail of the line approaching mistakenly thinking this was the rest of his fleet. It was in fact the first division of Boscawen's fleet. The second division had been ordered to pursue the remainder of La Clue's fleet and blockade them in port.

The British very quickly overhauled La Clue and in the ensuing action captured the French ship *Centaure*, however in this initial action Boscawen's flagship *Namur* was badly damaged. That evening La Clue's fleet scattered with two ships escaping out to sea and the remaining four being pursued next day and brought to action off the coast. Two French ships were wrecked being driven ashore and two more captured. Thus, the French Mediteranean fleet was neutralised and removed from the chess board in this most interesting and historical war of empire.

After the battle of Lagos in August invasion of England was out of the question but the French military still harboured designs on an invasion of Scotland using the transports assembled in the Gulf of Morbihan, the ones assembled near Vannes being unable to put to sea without escort. Admiral Sir Edward Hawke continued his blockade NNW of Ushant until the first week of November when it was blown back to the Channel taking refuge in Torbay leaving a small squadron under

Commodore Duff of five small sail of the line and nine frigates to watch the Gulf of Morbihan and the transports which were still rightly considered to be a threat.

As Hawke was forced back to Torbay and the gales subsided the French fleet under Admiral Conflans comprising twenty-one sail of the line and six frigates left Brest on the 14th November heading for the Gulf of Morbihan to collect the transports. On the 15th the fleet was spotted by a Royal Navy supply ship the *Love and Unity* seventy miles west of Belle Ille. This ship met with Hawke the following day, who had put back to sea after the gales, and passed on its vital intelligence to Hawke who set sail for Quiberon Bay hoping to intercept the French.

On the 19th Conflans was into Quiberon Bay and having spotted Duff's squadron gave chase. Duff scattered his fleet and headed out of the Bay to the NW with Conflans eagerly pursuing him when at eight thirty a.m. on the 20th, Conflans spotted Hawke closing in from the north into the bay. Conflans then turned about and headed back into the bay and into a brisk gale believing that Hawke would not dare follow into those treacherous waters in such poor conditions. He was wrong, in the finest traditions of the Royal Navy Hawke pursued Conflans into the bay. An interesting decision on Hawke's part and one which owes a great deal to the trial and execution of Admiral Byng some years earlier.

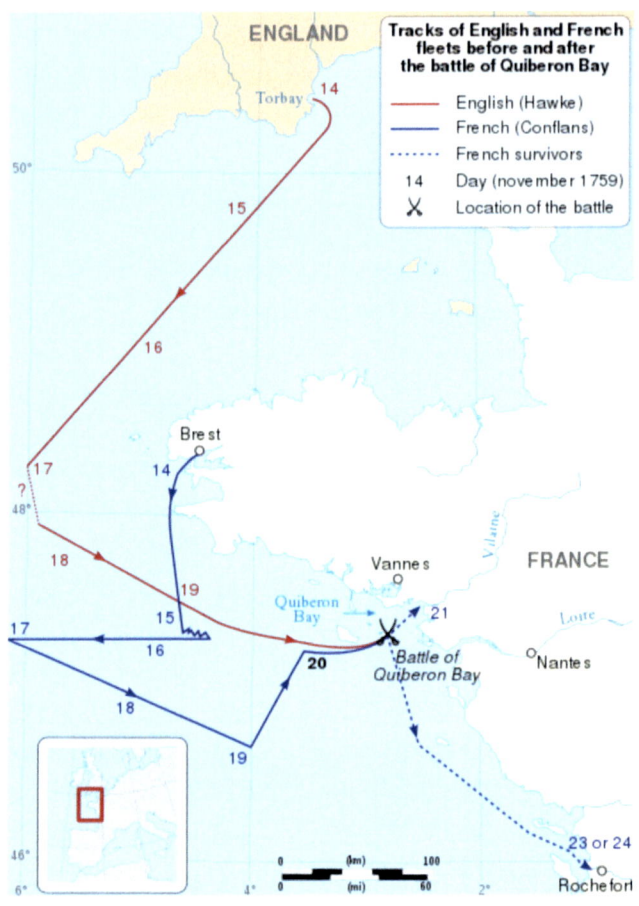

(Byng had been sent to reinforce Majorca but seeing the French fleet already besieging the island withdrew and was court-martialled for cowardice ironically in this particular instance doing more for the navy in death than in action.) Hawke believed that he could pursue and catch the French even at the expense of several ships foundering and not wishing to turn away and face the same consequences as Byng he swung into the bay and overtook the rear of the French line. At four p.m. the battered French ship of the line *Formidable* surrendered followed shortly after by the *Therese* and *Superbe*, the former foundering and the latter capsizing in the heavy seas. This was followed by the *Heros* which ran aground and surrendered before nightfall.

The night of the 20th saw Conflans attempting to escape Hawke by reforming the fleet and sailing out of the bay but sailing directly past the British fleet who raked the *Intrepid* causing severe damage. Both fleets then anchored that night and in the early gloom of the next day Conflans again attempted to run out of the bay but was pursued by the British where *HMS Essex* captured his flagship, however both ships ran aground on Four Sands.

The French fleet never recovered from these two British victories and played little part in the remainder of the Seven Years War. The French were unable to reinforce and supply their colonies in New France leading to the capture of those territories and most importantly of Quebec. The victory at Quiberon Bay was recognised as a key development in the continual building of the British Empire but I also believe that the Battle of Lagos should be included in this. As I stated earlier the two actions go together which leads on to my final observation regarding the French economy. There were also the devastating financial consequences of these defeats. In short financiers lost faith in France's ability to operate against the Royal Navy and protect trade. We also see the loss of two colonies in the Caribbean, Guadeloupe and Martinique. The result of this was the French Government defaulting on its debt causing huge financial turmoil.

The Saintes 1782

Surrender of Comte de Gosse to Rodney

The Battle of the Saintes is in my opinion one of the most important battles in naval history. It is often overshadowed by the previous events of the American Revolutionary War, events which resulted in the loss of all the thirteen colonies of the Americas and the rise of a new nation and the victory at Trafalgar twenty-three years later. The loss of the colonies was a bitter blow to Britain but they were still second in importance to the West Indies, the home of British prosperity. George III realised the importance of the islands and summed up the situation by declaring *'The West Indies must be defended, even at the risk of invasion of England'*. Loss of these important islands would have devastated the British economy and very likely stopped the empire in its tracks. A quarter of all imports to Britain (sugar) came from the West Indies, about £3m at that time and whole trading cities such as Liverpool and Glasgow relied on the carrying of that commodity across the Atlantic.

The battle was not just a famous victory for the Royal Navy at this time but it was also a proving ground for certain new inventions and innovations in naval warfare both in technological achievement and tactics. Let us first look at the technical innovations which would ultimately save the islands and the empire by considering a little-known figure in Royal Naval history. The Navy Controller at that time Charles Middleton (later Lord Barham and First Lord of the Admiralty). For my money equally as important as

Pepys for his administrative skills and industry but also for bringing to the Royal Navy the innovative upgrading of coppering and sheathing to British warships. All wooden vessels are subject to two great enemies at sea, ship worm and weed. Ship worm burrow deep into wooden hulls and eat their way through causing tremendous damage and weakening the frames of ships. Weed connects itself to wooden hulls and growing further slows down a ship's speed and lessens its manoeuvrability. This means that ships have to return to dry dock periodically especially when operating in tropical climates where the effects of worm and weed are far more virulent. There were no dry docks in the West Indies and now that America was gone the problem arose of how to keep a fleet at sea without a drydock facility. The answer was coppering the bottom of warships. A ship builder in the north west of England had contacted Middleton with a suggestion of coppering warships, as he had done for merchant ships sailing in African waters, a tried and tested method. Middleton was convinced of the need to carry out this upgrade and with the First Lord of the Admiralty Lord Sandwich he approached King George III directly with a scale model of a copper-bottomed ship and in turn convinced the king of the need to coat ships with this protective undercover. With the king's backing the Royal Navy went ahead coppering as many ships as possible and by 1782 the West Indies Squadron under Admiral Rodney was ready for action with this new technological advantage. To quote one Royal Navy Captain of its effects:

'The advantages from the helm alone is immense, as they feel them instantly, and wear in one third of the distance they ever did...'

Alongside this we see the invention of a new piece of ordnance for the Royal Navy. Visitors to *HMS Victory* at Portsmouth dockyard will have noticed on the top deck close to the front of the ship two squat cannons vastly different from the other guns on board. These are carronades. Named after the Carron Iron Foundry in Scotland where they were first designed and manufactured these are basically giant shotguns for close-in fighting. They fired a massive thirty-two pound shot which would sweep the decks of enemy ships taking dozens of men with them. This decisive weapon was soon replacing the smaller guns on top decks of warships and were carried in over half of Admiral Rodney's fleet at the Battle of the Saintes.

The second innovation was in tactics, quite simply the tactic of splitting the enemy line of battle. Until this time battles had been fought with ships in line astern in order to allow greater control and discipline and also to provide maximum firepower. However, there were drawbacks to this line of battle formation. One was that in making provision for the maximum use of the broadside one also made the ships susceptible to the enemy's equally damaging broadsides. This was countered to some extent by the rapid reloading of guns by the highly disciplined and experienced Royal Navy crews but still a danger. In addition to the line of battle and the fighting instructions which went alongside the tactic there was no real provision for independent thought and action by individual squadron commanders or captains and this made decisive conclusions to battles less likely. We would not see the full effects of breaking the enemy line until Trafalgar in 1805 but at the Saintes we see the beginnings of the tactic, a tactic which made full use of both the speed of ships due to coppering and the skill and aggression of Royal Navy personnel.

After the devastating loss of the American colonies not only was British confidence and moral at an all-time low but there now was a threat to the valuable colonies in the Caribbean. This was utmost in the minds of the British Government and steps needed to be taken to secure those colonies and win back the initiative in the region from the victorious French who were quite clearly going to exploit the situation further. To this end Admiral George Rodney was sent out from England with twelve sail of the line to reinforce the Royal Navy fleet in the region and to stop what were now known to be French plans to capture Jamaica.

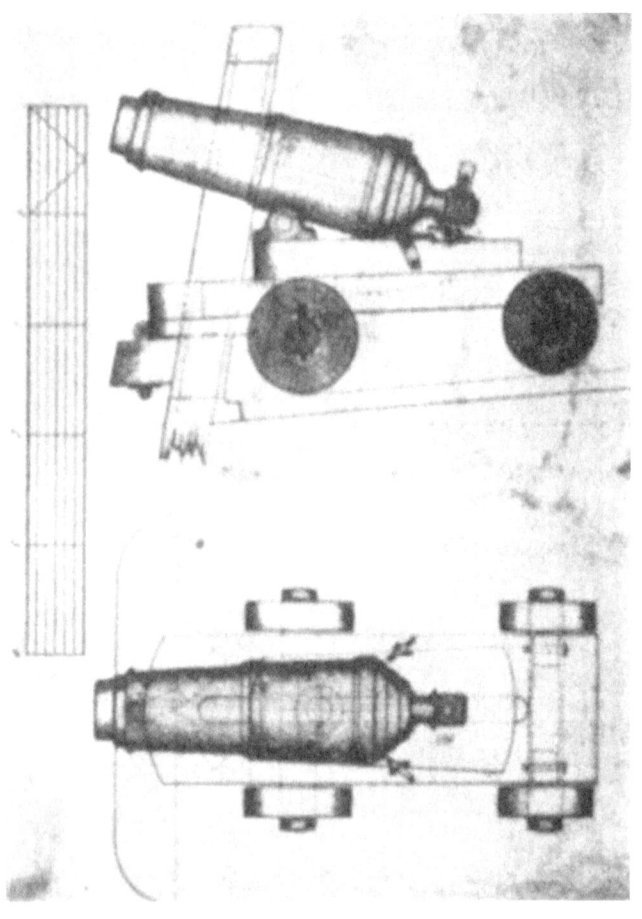

Carronade

Rodney arrived in mid-February 1782 to discover that several islands had already been taken by the French and the existing British fleet under the command of Admiral Hood was in a sorry state needing repairs and supplies, especially bread. Rodney immediately took charge and set about the two main tasks which he thought essential. Firstly, work needed be done to get Hood's fleet ready for action again as soon as possible. In order to achieve this as many repairs as were possible were carried out and more importantly the newly arrived British squadron under Rodney distributed as much of their supplies as they could among Hood's fleet. Second, was to prepare for the arrival of the French reinforcements for the fleet at Martinique and troops for capturing Jamaica.

Rodney split his force into three squadrons each of twelve sail of the line. Hood as Admiral of the Blue was sent to sit off Point Salines and cover those approaches, Vice Admiral Francis Drake as Admiral of the Red was to sit astride the sea between Point Salines and St Lucia. This covered all the southern approaches which were the most likely approaches to Martinique but crucially it left the northern routes clear. Hood several times pointed this out to Rodney and eventually Rodney sent a small detachment to cover the north but too late, the French reinforcements had already arrived. This was one of several clashes between Rodney and his second in command Hood and in this instance Hood's dismay at Rodney's lack of action to cover the north was a severe test of their relationship. In any event the French fleet under the Comte De Grasse was now at Fort Royal Martinique with thirty-six sail of the line and fifteen thousand troops ready for its attack on Jamaica. Having the French all in one place certainly made it easier to watch and then engage them as the British fleet could now be consolidated in one place but the failure to catch the French reinforcements was in my opinion a mixed blessing. The Royal Navy could have most certainly caught and captured the squadron possibly before the main French fleet came out but it would have meant dividing the fleet even further and had the French come out to assist the approaching reinforcements a large portion of the British fleet could have been destroyed. But the loss of those six thousand troops and the siege equipment could have meant that the French could not invest Jamaica and the whole project would have been stillborn. However, on the plus side it meant that the French were now all together, would have to come out and could be engaged and defeated, permanently removing any threat to the British possessions in the Caribbean. Had the reinforcements been stopped the French would still be sat there tying up an entire British fleet which would be steadily decaying and without the use of a dry dock facility so perhaps '*all's well that ends well*'.

On 5th April, the French fleet set sail from Fort Royal heading north to collect more troops from Guadeloupe then west to Jamaica. Rodney immediately set off in pursuit and the speed of his ships due to the coppering and sheathing allowed him to catch up and by the 9th April, the two fleets were in sight of each other. Unfortunately, the winds dropped as night approached and only a desultory action took place that day. The 10th April was spent by both fleets trying to work to windward, a long and laborious process at very low speeds, probably only two or three knots so again no major action ensued that day but what was clear was that the French were trying to avoid battle. Not surprising and certainly not cowardly in any way. The French had a plan which was to land an army, engaging a British fleet must come second to that and most importantly the ships were crowded with troops making them harder to manage and putting the troops in extreme danger. Despite De Grasse's best attempts he could not outrun the British ships and battle was becoming increasingly likely. As dawn broke on the 11th, the French fleet was still well to windward of the British fleet but Rodney was catching them. Two French ships the *Zele* and *Magnanime* had fallen astern of the French fleet and Rodney decided to seize the chance of engaging them in the hope that De Grasse would turn around and come back to protect them, which he did leaving the scene set for a major engagement the next day the 12th April.

The morning of the 12th April saw the two opposing fleets in the waters to the north of Dominica near a group of islands known as the Saintes with the French proceeding on a southerly course and the British on a northerly approaching each other at around five or six knots. Rodney seeing the French fleet ordered line ahead and changed course to the north east to close the gap and engage, the fleets finally converging at around eight a.m. when the lead ship in the British line, *HMS Marlborough* opened fire followed by the rest of the line who exchanged fire with the French fleet. Rodney's flagship *HMS Formidable* at one time shortened sail in the action in order to concentrate on De Grasse's flagship the large first-rate sail of the line *Ville De Paris*. The battle was developing into a typical line astern battle at this stage and had it continued so may well have been inconclusive but at around nine a.m. the wind suddenly shifted to the south causing the French ships to bear away to the south west. This caused gaps to open in the French line and these were subsequently exploited by the British. It is unknown who gave the order for the ships to split the line of the French fleet, there are no records of Rodney giving such an order so it is safe to assume that individual captains took advantage of the situation and sailed between the French ships in three places. It transpires, that four French ships fouled each other, and got entangled allowing a gap to form either side of them and this was exploited by Rodney in the *Formidable* who broke the line and raked the French ships as he passed, soon followed by the rest of the squadron who simply followed Rodney. The change of wind direction and the subsequent breaking of the line caused confusion among the French ships which taken aback were soon being raked by the British ships in quick succession. The decks crowded with soldiers and stores for the invasion soon became a virtual hell on earth of flying splinters, grapeshot and decks awash with blood.

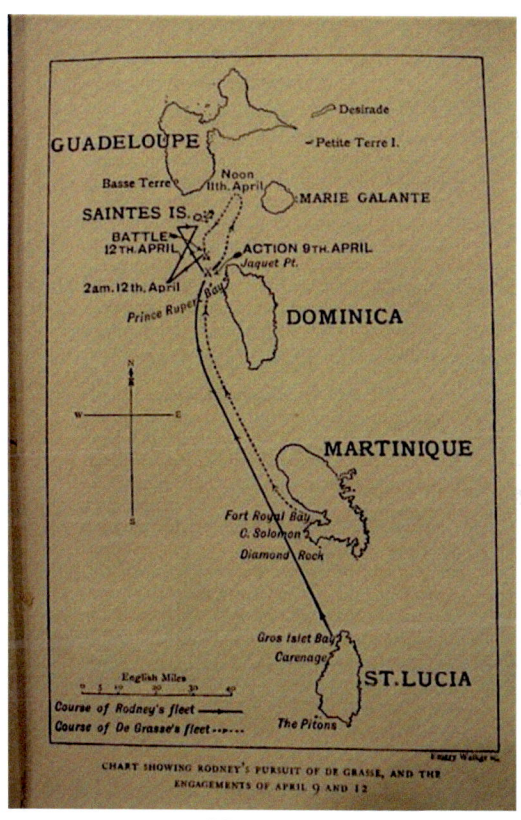

Map of fleet movements

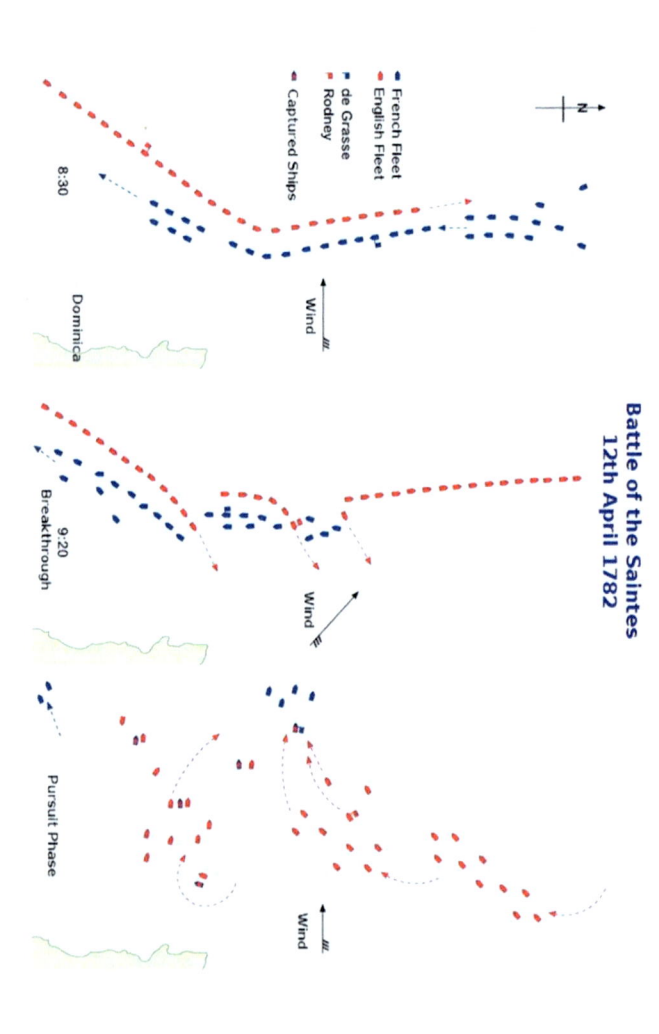

At around mid-morning the wind dropped again causing a brief lull in the battle and giving time for minor repairs but at noon the wind picked up again and Rodney was able to turn and pursue the French to the south west, again his faster ships catching the rear guard. The first French ship to haul down it's colours in surrender was the seventy-four gun third rate *Cesar* followed at four thirty p.m. by the seventy-four gun *Hector*. At six p.m. the sixty-four gun *Ardent* (formerly a Royal Navy ship captured in 1779) struck her colours and this was probably the most significant victory of the day as she contained the French army siege train. This was soon followed by the capture of De Grasse and his flagship the *Ville De Paris* which marked the end of the day's action.

The French losses were significant, not only had the fleet taken a pounding but five sail of the line had been taken including the flagship and Admiral De Grasse but also the siege train. On top of this there were reported to be around seven thousand five hundred troops killed which with the loss of the siege train and the battering of the fleet made any enterprise to capture Jamaica impossible. However, the battle was not yet over. Hood's squadron had not been engaged in the battle and was therefore in good shape so Rodney sent him to sit off the Mona Straits near St Domingo to catch any French ships trying to seek shelter after the battle. This was proved to be a good move as Hood was able to capture a further four ships bringing the total losses to seven sail of the line, one frigate and one sloop captured.

This was certainly a decisive victory and secured the Caribbean for Britain, a most important act, but it was also crowded in controversy. Admiral Hood, who was not enamoured with his commander, publicly and privately criticised Rodney for not ordering a general chase when the wind picked up at noon on the 12th, believing that had he done so more French ships would have been captured. We will never know of course but it seems likely that a general chase would have resulted in more ships captured rather than Rodney's continued line astern formation which limits ships to the speed of the lead ship. However, for all said and done a great victory had been achieved, prestige and confidence put back into the Royal Navy and most importantly the rich possessions of the Caribbean secured. In spite of Hood's criticisms of Rodney he was to write to the First Lord of the Admiralty Lord Sandwich that:

'I have the honour and pleasure to acquaint your lordship that his majesty's fleet has given such a beating to that of France as no great fleet ever had before.'

This was echoed by Rodney who later wrote to Lord Sandwich:

'I flatter myself I shall soon have an opportunity of congratulating your lordship upon Jamaica being out of danger.'

The French Admiral De Grasse, a very capable man, had been taken and his fleet shattered along with nine thousand dead and wounded and over half his invasion army lost. In total nine French ships had been destroyed or captured during the battle and the days following. The Saintes was a decisive victory for Rodney and the Royal Navy. It had saved Jamaica and the West Indies and therefore saved the empire and Britain itself. The Royal Navy was once again dominant and the French monarchy was now in serious danger, having spent so much on the navy with no return the cost to the nation was enormous and the consequent economic backlash would lead eventually to revolution and another war.

Trafalgar 1805

Certainly, the most famous naval battle in history Trafalgar has earnt almost mythical status as a decisive battle at sea which brought fame and glory to both the Royal Navy and Admiral Horatio Nelson. There is so much to talk about with this battle it is a challenge to know where to begin as the foundations for this great victory actually go back over a century before the event with the evolution of the Royal Navy to the finely honed weapon it had become by 1805. As we saw in the previous chapter technological innovation had given the Royal Navy a decisive edge over the French fleet at The Saintes leading to a great victory that had restored British prestige and confidence and saved a valuable part of the empire from capture. But for all this it was still not an annihilation of an enemy fleet and from the beginning of the following wars with France which started in 1793 we see this pattern in almost every encounter. Up to 1805 the Royal Navy had defeated the French and Spanish navies several times in large fleet actions but had not inflicted major losses on the enemy. Battles were won and the seas retained for Britain but always there lurked the constant threat of an enemy fleet in being which had to be watched and guarded against. At the Battle of the Nile in 1798 we do see what I call an annihilation of a small French fleet when Nelson caught the fleet that had brought Napoleon to Egypt and destroyed or captured ten out of twelve sail of the line, an immense victory for its time proving that it can be achieved and this was not lost on Nelson. Nelson's ambition was to bring the French and Spanish fleets to battle and destroy them thus removing the threat of invasion of Britain once and for all.

In 1803 war broke out again between Britain and France after the short-lived peace of Amiens and the Royal Navy once again took up its customary duty of blockading the enemy in port. Key to this strategy was the blockading of Brest by Admiral Cornwallis and of the French Mediterranean fleet in Toulon by Admiral Nelson. During the peace of Amiens Napoleon had been giving much thought and planning as to how he could knock Britain and her all powerful navy out of the war for good and decided that the only course of action was to invade Britain. Napoleon was no doubt a military genius but his knowledge and confidence stopped where land ended and his somewhat half conceived plan was for the French fleets to leave port, join up with their Spanish Allies and sail to the West Indies to raid shipping, thus drawing off the Royal Navy in pursuit. Once this had been achieved the fleet would then sail back to the English Channel and collect the French Army mustering near Boulogne and deliver it to southern England. In Napoleon's eyes a perfectly simple and workable plan but was the French fleet up to it? I cannot find any records to suggest that Napoleon intended to meet the Royal Navy in open battle and defeat them and my thoughts are that this was never the intention, the plan was clearly to draw off the Royal Navy long enough to land the army in Kent but as events were to show this was not possible although the plan did almost succeed. The one factor that Napoleon did not anticipate was that he assumed that both British fleets would pursue the combined fleet from the Mediterranean and the Channel, however this was never the case, Cornwallis would never leave his station, it was far too important a strategic deployment and this is where the plan starts to fall apart for Napoleon.

In January 1805 a French squadron managed to leave Rochefort evading the British blockade and set sail for the West Indies. This was followed by the French fleet leaving Toulon under Admiral Villeneuve at the end of March. How did he evade Nelson's blockade? Blockading is not as easy as it sounds. It must be remembered that the wind that allows a fleet to leave harbour will also drive out to sea any ships patrolling outside and Nelson did make one error of judgement in that his main fleet was not outside Toulon, he was only watching the port with a few frigates. A week after the French left Toulon the Spanish fleet left Cadiz and it was not until the 10th April that Nelson learnt that the bird had flown and passed through the Straits of Gibraltar. When further intelligence arrived with Nelson that the combined Franco-Spanish fleet was headed for the West Indies he belatedly gave chase but by this time was some weeks behind Villeneuve. Stage one of Napoleon's plan seemed to have worked but only partly as Cornwallis remained where he was blockading Brest. Villeneuve a brave and capable admiral was under no illusions that he could face a Royal Navy fleet in battle and win. The Royal Navy had been at sea outside French and Spanish ports for months if not years constantly beating back and forth in all weathers and carrying out gun drill until they could load and fire every three minutes and sometimes within ninety seconds with extreme accuracy. The French and Spanish had been languishing in port unable to carry out gun or sail drill so a confrontation was not in Villeneuve's best interests. In view of this it appears that Villeneuve lost his nerve to some extent and hearing that Nelson was on his way he prematurely vacated the Indies without actually engaging at all, so a unique opportunity to train the crews and give them some combat experience was thus lost.

Heading back to the Channel as ordered Villeneuve encountered a small British squadron off Cape Finisterre on 22nd July 1805. The Royal Navy was heavily outgunned and outnumbered but this spirited action by Admiral Calder and subsequent victory was to lay the foundations for the later victory at Trafalgar. Calder managed to engage Villeneuve and capture two ships and this seems to have added to Villeneuve's already rampant pessimism and caused him to abandon the plan and head south to seek safety in Cadiz where by mid- August the combined fleet was again blockaded in port. A furious Napoleon realising that any invasion attempt was now out of the question decided to move his army east to confront the Austrians and Russians. The immediate threat to Britain had been removed but with the still large combined fleet in being the threat of invasion still remained.

By late September Nelson was off Cadiz with his fleet fully expecting Villeneuve to come out, not to give battle but more likely to run south back into the

Mediterranean and he was proved absolutely right. Napoleon dismayed at the actions of his admiral had decided to replace Villeneuve and when news of this reached the French Admiral in Cadiz he decided to take the combined fleet back in to the Mediterranean and regain some of the lost confidence of Napoleon, though quite how I do not know. This smacks of a desperate attempt to gain some favour by doing something rather than nothing and does fit with Villeneuve's character as an honourable man and certainly no coward. Nelson convinced that Villeneuve would have to come out had already designed his plan of battle and at a dinner on board his flagship *HMS Victory* on the night of the 29th September he confided and explained this plan to his captains. Initially they were shocked at such bold tactics which envisaged the fleet attacking at right angles to the enemy, cutting their line of battle in two places thus allowing enemy ships to be raked from stem to stern preparatory to boarding. Nelson explained that a great deal depended on individual ships engaging enemy ships in a pell-mell battle but he concluded by telling his captains. '*No captain can do very wrong if he places his ship alongside that of an enemy.*' Such tactics of course were not new, the same had been attempted and used in previous battles to great success the most recent being the Battle of Camperdown when a Dutch fleet was captured. But the plan was risky. Advancing on an enemy's line of battle at near right angles meant that the lead ships would be exposed to enemy fire without the ability to fire back. However, Nelson counted on two things to alleviate what appears to be a disadvantageous situation. Firstly, he believed that after weeks in port and no gunnery practice the enemy fleet would not be able to fire accurately and with speed. Secondly, in the traditional practice of the French and Spanish they would aim for the sails and rigging so if men stayed below decks they would not be harmed and with a prevailing wind the speed of ships not diminished too much. Nelson also judged that splitting the line would allow the British to cut off the van of the combined fleet which would take a long time to beat back and take part in the battle. In actual fact the first two or three ships of each column did suffer damage but no ship was put out of action or lost.

Villeneuve had fought Nelson before at the Nile in 1798 and was very confident in the tactics that Nelson would employ. He had surmised very accurately that Nelson would not be in line of battle and that he would attempt to break the combined fleet's line in probably several places leading to individual engagements where the Royal Navy would show its superiority over the untrained and inexperienced French and Spanish crews

On 19th October 1805 the frigate *HMS Sirius* patrolling outside Cadiz hoisted the signal '*enemy ships are coming out of port*'. This signal was repeated and relayed by frigates for forty-eight miles out to sea to Nelson's waiting fleet and at nine thirty a.m. Nelson ordered a general chase to the south east. The chess pieces were being placed. The southerly wind made it a certainty that the British fleet would intercept the combined fleet before they reached Gibraltar and as dawn broke on the 21st October Nelson could see the combined fleet heading on a course of south, south, east at a forty-five-degree angle to his advance. He immediately ordered deployment and preparation for battle. Villeneuve realising that he would not make it to the Straits of Gibraltar ordered the fleet to return to Cadiz. This manoeuvre caused confusion among the fleet and a valuable two hours was lost in reforming the line (which did not reform properly) allowing the British to make certain of their interception of the combined fleet. On board the British ships which were approaching the enemy at about two knots there was ample time for the crews to have breakfast and lunch as well as the very welcome pre battle tot of rum when at eleven fifteen a.m. Nelson hoisted his famous signal *'England expects that every man shall do his duty'*. This was followed shortly after by signal number 16 in the signal book *'close action'*.

The Battle of Trafalgar, Turner

The Franco-Spanish line was first split by the division under Nelson's deputy Admiral Collingwood who sailed his flagship the *Royal Sovereign* neatly between the French *Fougueux* and Spanish *Santa Anna* the eighteenth ship in the line, raking both ships with double-shotted salvos as she passed through causing much carnage and damage. *Royal Sovereign* was then followed by the remaining ships in the division and from the deck of the *Victory* all Nelson could see was a smoke shrouded melee just as he had anticipated. Nelson in the *Victory* engaged the combined fleet at around twelve forty-five p.m. sailing between the *Bucanteaur* and *Redoutable* followed by the remainder of his division. It was whilst engaged alongside the *Redoutable* that the fateful musket ball entered Nelson's body lodging itself in his chest. He was carried below to a painful death unable to take part in the reminder of the battle but this is where we see the professionalism of the Royal Navy coming to the fore. The great leader was down but the battle continued as each man in the fleet knew his duty and direction was no longer needed or in fairness of any use. It was every ship for itself as in turn each Royal Navy ship of the line came alongside a French or Spanish ship and successfully raked and boarded it. Nelson by a supreme marshalling of iron will in what must have been an agonising death remained long enough to hear from his flag captain Thomas Hardy that a great victory had been achieved and that fifteen of the enemy had been taken. Satisfied at last the great man breathed his final words, *'Thank God I have done my duty'*, and died in the arms of his dear friend Hardy. The entry in Victory's log sums up the battle very neatly. *'Partial firing continued until four thirty p.m., when a victory having been reported to the Right Honourable Lord Viscount Nelson, KB and Commander in Chief, died of his wounds'*.

One of the most informative contemporary summaries of the battle comes from the captain of the frigate, *HMS Euryalus*, which common with ships of that size had not taken part in the battle. Watching events from a safe distance captain Blackwood was to write: *'Almost all seemed as if inspired by the one common sentiment of conquer or die. The enemy, to do them justice, were not less so. They waited the attack of the British with a coolness I was sorry to witness and they fought in a way that must do them honour'.*

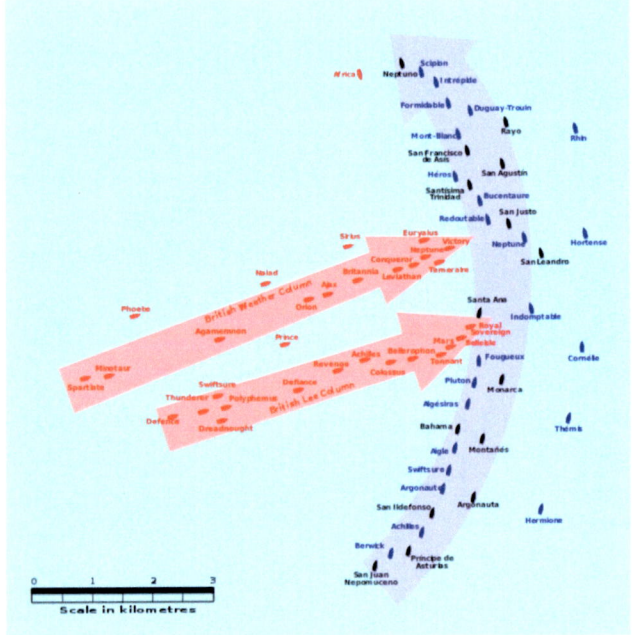

Map of fleet movements

The victory of Trafalgar was an annihilation. Eighteen enemy ships had been taken and eleven so badly battered that they would not sail again. This last great victory of the age of sail was to give the Royal Navy a primacy in the world that would go unchallenged for over one hundred years.

Tsushima 1905

Admiral Togo on the deck of the Mikasa

Like Trafalgar this battle was to have far reaching consequences and victory in the Russo-Japanese War for Japan would provide a visible realignment between the two worlds of oriental and occidental. Ever since the opening up of Japan to the western world by the *'Black Ships'* sent to Japan in 1853 (a US battle fleet sent to intimidate Japan into opening the country to trade) Japan had been pulling herself out of the feudal society she had lived under for centuries and into the modern world. Samurai warriors set aside their swords in exchange for rifles and above all warships and in the following fifty years we see an ever more aggressive, imperialist and ambitious Japan forcing herself on firstly Asian countries and then with the coming of war with Russia in 1905 against a large imperial European power.

Russia at the turn of the last century was huge and albeit industrially and economically somewhat backward still a formidable empire with vast resources for war. Russia was considered a major threat to the British Empire with her cloak and dagger meddling in the north west frontier region of India and Afghanistan and an ever-growing powerful fleet which presented a real threat in northern waters. Always ambitious and constantly looking for expansion Russia despite her size and spanning such a vast landmass of the world lacked one vital ingredient in further expansion and that was warm water ports that opened into the Pacific and Indian Oceans. Her constant attempts to influence Afghanistan were a clear attempt at gaining a port in Persia and what is now Pakistan but it is the Far East that we must concern ourselves with for the purposes of this narrative.

The one Pacific port that Russia had was Vladivostok but this was only available in the summer months, being ice bound the remainder of the year so a deal was struck with China to lease Port Arthur to the west of the Korean peninsula. The Russians based their

1st Pacific Squadron there and fortified the city against land and sea attack. The possession of this vital port allowed Russia to influence the region and her designs on Korea and Manchuria were a strong basis for her foreign policy in Asia. It was always inevitable that Russia and Japan would eventually lock horns over the region but Russia had always been confident in the knowledge that a modern European power had never been bested by an Asian power in battle and who in their right mind would take on the might of holy Russia?

Japan ever fearful of Russian encroachment and conscious of her own ambitions decided to approach Russia with what they hoped was an equally beneficial arrangement whereby Russia could have dominance over Manchuria if Japan could have a free hand in Korea. Russia refused insisting that the area of Korea north of the 39th parallel just above Seoul be a buffer zone between Russia and Japan. This was a blatant attempt to stop any further expansion by Japan and was refused accordingly leading Japan to seek what she wanted with war. The parallels to me between this period and the road to war in 1941 are startling and speak much for the attitude of Japan in the first half of the 20th century. When negotiations broke down in 1941 Japan went to war with little notice and no legal declaration and in 1904, we see the exact same sequence of events. From the late 19th century to the end of World War II, I see Japan as an infant alligator trying to hatch out of its shell, writhing its head and snapping its jaws at all around it desperate to get out and start life afresh. On the 8th February 1904, and after having declared war a bare three hours earlier Japan's navy attacked the Russian fleet in Port Arthur.

On the night of the 8th February Japanese torpedo boats entered the harbour at Port Arthur and attacked the Russian fleet at anchor, badly damaging two of the most modern battleships in the Russian Navy as well as a cruiser. This attack was the first event in what was to become known, as the Battle of Port Arthur, a series of naval attacks by Japan to neutralise the Russian fleet all of which were beaten off by the shore batteries protecting Port Arthur and culminating in two attempts to sink ships in the harbour entrance to seal the port and trap the fleet but these failed as the ships were sunk too far offshore.

The Russians although safe in port realised that they could not stay there indefinitely and should try and break out in order to join up with the squadron at Vladivostok so on the 12th April flying his flag in the battleship *Petropavlosk* Admiral Makarov attempted a breakout but was forced back into port after two of his battleships hit mines. Unfortunately for Russia, Makarov was killed when his flagship sunk. Naval losses were evened up however when on the 15th May two Japanese battleships sunk after hitting mines just outside the harbour.

With the appointment of Admiral Vitgeft to command the Russian fleet at Port Arthur it was hoped that further aggressive attempts to break out would be made but Vitgeft was reluctant to do so. At this time Russian naval policy was to keep the fleet in being and Vitgeft believed that his ships could be of more use assisting in the defence of Port Arthur against the besieging Japanese Army but Tsar Nicholas ordered him to break out and reach Vladivostok which Vitgeft attempted to do leading to the Battle of the Yellow Sea.

At 09.55 am on the 10th August 1904, the Russian fleet cleared Port Arthur and headed on a south easterly course to round the headland and head for Vladivostok. It was a formidable fleet consisting of six battleships, four protected cruisers (partially armoured decking) and fourteen destroyers. This fleet was intercepted at 12.25pm by the Japanese fleet under Admiral Togo consisting of five battleships, ten armoured cruisers (similar to protected cruisers but with a band of armour along the sides), eighteen destroyers and thirty torpedo boats. Long range fire commenced at about one p.m. and after three hours the Russian fleet turned back for Port Arthur having lost Admiral Vitgeft in the action. No ships were lost by either side but each fleet pounded the other scoring numerous hits at quite long ranges. All eyes were on this theatre of war as navies around the world wanted to see how large gunned armoured ships performed in battle against each other, this was the first chance to see which weapons worked and which did not, which guns were better and above all which ship designs were better.

With the Russian fleet bottled up in Port Arthur and the port under siege from the Japanese Army the war was not going Russia's way so the momentous decision was made to send the Baltic fleet under Admiral Rozhestvensky eighteen thousand miles around the world to link up with the fleets in Port Arthur and Vladivostok, bring the Japanese to battle and overwhelm them. This was a monumental task thought to be pure lunacy in most quarters but was actually the only successful part of the Russian war. The fleet consisting of eleven battleships, eight cruisers and nine destroyers left the Baltic on the 15th October 1904 to begin its seven-month voyage but almost immediately caused controversy when sailing over the Dogger Bank the trigger happy and nervous Russian gunners mistook the British fishing fleets for Japanese torpedo boats and opened fire sinking at least one fishing boat and in the confusion firing on each other. This caused a serious diplomatic incident with Britain and matters looked as though they would get quickly out of hand when the Royal Navy battlefleet of twenty-eight battleships and supporting ships was ordered into the North Sea. War did not break out with Britain of course but the Russian Navy was shadowed by the Royal Navy all the way to the coast of Portugal, possibly passing on intelligence to their Japanese Allies.

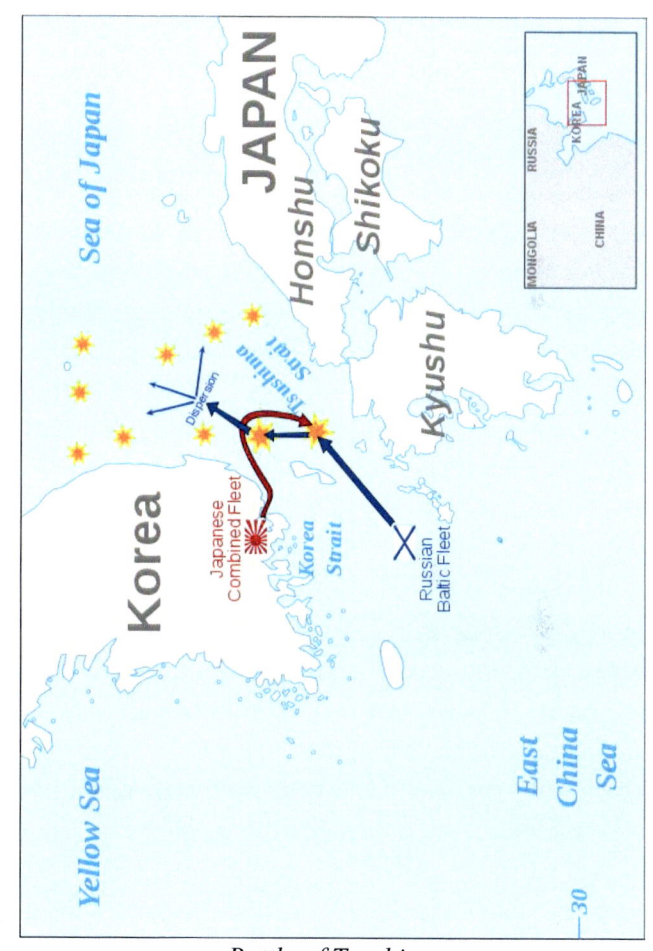

Battle of Tsushima

The Russian fleet finally arrived off the Sea of Japan in May 1905 but the situation had changed since they left. Port Arthur had fallen and the entire Russian Pacific fleet had been forced to surrender. Rozhestvensky's only course of action was to now head for Vladivostok and link up with the cruisers there. On the night of the 26th/27th May the Russian fleet approached the Straits of Tsushima and under cover of a thick fog and away from the more popular sea lanes tried to sneak through into the Sea of Japan headed for Vladivostok. At two forty-five a.m. the Japanese cruiser *Shinaro Maru* spotted three lights in the distance and set off to investigate. The three lights belonged to the Russian hospital ship *Orel* who in line with international law was correctly displaying the lights to denote that she was a hospital ship. However, the captain of the *Orel* went a step further in breaking the fleet's concealment by signalling to the Japanese cruiser that there were Russian ships nearby, a serious error as he believed that the Japanese cruiser was Russian. The *Shinaro Mura* immediately telegraphed Admiral Togo the commander of the Japanese fleet and continued to monitor the course and speed of the Russian fleet until Togo left harbour at just after six thirty a.m. on the 27th May heading north east on an intercept course. At two forty-five p.m. the Japanese fleet intercepted the Russian's and Togo ordered line astern in order to cross the Russian T and cut them off from continuing north, this was followed by a turn to the west pounding the Russian ships all the while. Togo then formed into a parallel line and continued to exchange fire as the fleets headed north east. At around five p.m. the Russians again turned north in an attempt to head for Vladivostok but the Japanese stuck with them causing huge damage. One of the most accurate contemporary narratives of the battle is from Commander Vladimir Semenoff, a Russian staff officer aboard the flagship *Knyaz Suvorov* who said of the battle: *"It seemed impossible even to count the number of projectiles striking us. Shells seemed to be pouring upon us incessantly one after another. The steel plates and superstructure on the upper decks were torn to pieces, and the splinters caused many casualties. Iron ladders were crumpled up into rings, guns were literally hurled from their mountings. In addition to this, there was the unusually high temperature and liquid flame of the explosion, which seemed to spread over everything. I actually watched a steel plate catch fire from a burst."*

The Russians were also achieving hits on the Japanese ships but there were crucial differences. The Japanese shells were high explosive and were causing huge destruction to the superstructures of the Russian ships whereas the Russian ships were using armour piercing shells. These kind of shells, were just as destructive as the high explosive but many failed to explode on contact. Also, in a sinister glimpse into the future where similar circumstances would be seen again at Jutland in 1916, we see the Russian decks still loaded with coal which soon ignited adding to the damage caused. Under the constant and accurate bombardment, the Russian ships began to founder one by one.

At 3.50 p.m. the Russian battleship *Oslyabya* sunk, earning the unfortunate reputation of being the first modern battleship to be sunk by gunfire. This was followed shortly after by the *Borodino, Knyaz Suvorov* and *Imperator Alekandr III*, all battleships. By 6.20 p.m. night was beginning to fall and Togo launched his second offensive of that day by sending in his torpedo boats from the south and east and his destroyers from the north to finish off the battered Russian fleet. This attack caused the fleet to break apart and individual groups of Russian ships tried independently to reach Vladivostock. Time ran out though for two more Russian battleships, the *Navarin* which struck a mine and was later sunk by torpedoes and the *Sissoi Veliky* which was also torpedoed and scuttled the next day. In addition to the battleship losses two armoured cruisers were also scuttled after being badly damaged. Battle commenced again on the 28th May with Togo's battleships surrounding what was left of the Russian fleet and pounding it from twelve thousand metres. At this range the Russians could not respond as their guns did not have the range and Admiral Nebogatov (in command after Rozhestvensky was wounded in the earlier action) decided enough was enough and to surrender. This leads to one of the most tragic incidents of the battle, indeed if it were not for the subsequent death and carnage it could even be laughable.

Nebogatov ordered the hoisting of signal XGE, the internationally recognised signal of surrender. Togo however kept firing. Not a cruel sadistic act on his part but extraordinarily simply because the Japanese did not understand the signal not having the word surrender in their signal book! Attempts to raise white flags on the Russian ships were also ignored as the Chinese had tried this before with Togo and deceived him so it was not until the Japanese imperial flag was hoisted on Russian ships that the Japanese ceased fire. Russian losses were huge, eleven battleships sunk, captured or scuttled along with four cruisers and six destroyers. Japanese losses were three torpedo boats.

What had led to this stunning victory? Japanese gunnery was simply superior, the shells better and the guns had longer range. In addition to this the range finding equipment was far more effective than the Russian's. The Japanese crews were highly trained with officers being taught by Royal Navy officers and to cap it all the crews had combat experience. Only three ships reached Vladivostok and very soon the Russian nation was calling for peace, a peace which the Tsar had to reluctantly agree to as the internal dissent was too strong to ignore in Russia.

For me this battle is significant as it was the first battle fought by armoured big gunned battleships. It is singularly exceptional due to the fantastic odyssey of the Russian fleet sailing around the world to the Sea of

Japan, a stunning achievement worthy of the greatest respect. But above all I see here the beginning of the road to Pearl Harbour. Japanese aggression and ambition could not be checked by Russia and this victory would provide what the Japanese considered a virtual suit of armour giving confidence to their imperial drive in the region. After World War I had beaten the European nations into the ground Japan saw herself as all powerful in the Far East and it was a very short step from victory over Russia in 1905 to the invasion of China in 1937 and thence to Pearl Harbour.

For Russia the war proved ultimately disastrous. The strong warlike Germans and Central Powers saw Russia as weak and obsolete and this may well have contributed to their pugnacious attitude leading up to World War I having apparently nothing to fear from Russia.

Jutland 1916

HMS Iron Duke

The Battle of Jutland was a fascinating battle in many respects. Firstly, it represented the last major confrontation of surface fleets without the aid of aircraft carriers, secondly it was an important battle in that for the first time, heavy dreadnought class battleships had faced each other. Looking back to the days of sail one could safely predict that British seamanship, gunnery and boarding would win the day against French and Spanish ships. However, in the dreadnought age the chances of carrying an action by boarding would not be an option. As we shall discover gunnery was of importance in the way in which guns were managed. In the age of sail where the British Navy fired three broadsides to every one of the enemy at close range, the effect was devastating. However, in the age of dreadnoughts the rate of fire was not only less important as opposed to accuracy, but was to prove fatal to British warships.

Let us first look at the development of both the dreadnought and the use of blue water navies prior to WWI. In 1904 a new First Sea Lord took up his post in the Admiralty. He had served in *HMS Warrior* during the 1860s and was an expert in the use of torpedoes, thus he had a good grasp of modern technology and was to prove instrumental in the development of two classes of warship which would take their place in the annals of naval history, and contribute in their own way to the outbreak of war. His name was Sir John Arbuthnot Fisher. Jacky Fisher. Certainly, an eccentric man but most importantly a radical man for significant times, Fisher was to change history and keep Britain the most powerful naval force in the world for the next fifteen years.

His first task in taking on his new role was to look at the Royal Navy dispositions throughout the empire and deploy his forces in the most efficient and strategic manor. This had to be done as a new menace was arising from across the North Sea in the shape of Germany, who under the leadership of the Kaiser and Admiral Tirpitz was threatening the Royal Navy in its own back yard. How can Britain retain the most powerful navy in the world if it cannot control home waters? This was the problem which faced Fisher. So he did three things. Fisher pushed for and achieved alliances with the empire of Japan and France. This allowed the second plan to be implemented which was bring home units of the fleet and either scrap outdated warships or bolster the home fleet. The treaties with Japan and France meant that a number of large ships could come home providing crews for the ever-larger vessels being built. Thirdly he went on to implement the design of a new class of warship to beat all others. The dreadnought class.

In 1905 Japan and Russia went to war. The land campaign was fairly evenly matched but at sea Japan was in the ascendant. During the Battle of the Straits of Tsushima the Japanese fleet under Admiral Togo destroyed a larger Russian battle fleet which had sailed all the way from the Baltic, thus sealing the fate of Port Arthur and ultimately winning the war. The battle was important to observers at the time as it showed how the battleships competed and what the weapons did to armour plate. The Royal Navy consensus was that in the modern sea battle it was big guns that counted. The large ten and twelve inch guns performed very well firing with a flatter trajectory and causing serious damage after penetration. The smaller calibre guns of four, five, six and eight inches just did not count against battleships as the shells caused little damage or were of insufficient range. This vital intelligence caused Fisher to undertake the most radical designing of a warship since the *Warrior*. The result was *HMS Dreadnought* launched in 1906. She was superior in every way to any previous steam warship. She bristled with armament carrying ten, twelve inch guns in five turrets as well many smaller calibre guns (added later to deal with destroyers). She used steam turbines giving her a top speed of over twenty knots (about eight knots faster than existing battleships). *Dreadnought* could both outrun and outgun any existing warship in the world. However, as a consequence *Dreadnought* made every other battleship virtually obsolete overnight, including those of the Royal Navy. This allowed her arch rival Germany to believe she could catch up in the naval arms race. In addition to the dreadnoughts the battle cruiser was also designed. This was not a particularly successful warship as it was never properly used for its intended purpose which was to scout ahead of the main fleet and sink enemy cruiser scouts. Battle cruisers were armed with the same amount and calibre of guns as dreadnoughts, however they were considerably faster having sacrificed armour for speed. This meant that taking their place in the line of battle they were extremely vulnerable to the high calibre plunging shot of battleships.

Kaiser Wilhelm II was obsessed with the sea. As a child he was seen and pictured many times in a sailor's uniform. He was an Admiral of the Fleet in the Royal Navy, and as the grandson of Queen Victoria he had seen what the Royal Navy had done for Britain and how it had built the empire. Germany in 1885 was a militaristic country, however this was built on an impressive and successful army. What the Kaiser understood was that if one is to build an empire, (and that was certainly his intention) one must have a navy to protect it. You cannot have one without the other. The problem was how do you convince an almost landlocked nation that its future lay in the sea? This was a most monumental task but was achieved brilliantly by both the Kaiser and the Minister of Marine Admiral Tirpitz with a program of education which convinced the Germans that a navy was both needed and could be used. Thus, Germany began embarking on building a navy to rival its maritime neighbours, and cause questions to be raised in parliament in Britain. Fisher's response was simple. Britain will out-build Germany. In the standing joke of the time 'The Admiralty asked for six dreadnoughts a year, the Treasury offered four, so they settled on eight'. Eight was something that Germany just could not compete with. At the outbreak of war Britain had twenty dreadnoughts with a further twelve under construction, Germany had fifteen and six under construction.

Tirpitz realised that the Imperial German Navy could never defeat the Royal Navy in an open battle, and in fairness this was never his intention. However, what the German Navy could do (according to Alfred Mahan) was apply something called risk theory. Essentially this meant that all the German Navy had to do was provide a large enough threat to the Royal Navy in its own backyard so to speak. This would mean that should war occur, the British would either have to station such large numbers of ships in home waters or suffer such losses at sea in a battle (albeit at the potential destruction of the German fleet) that she could not protect her empire and its sea lanes from other enemies. Therefore, Britain would not dare fight the German Navy. Risk theory. Dangerous, but not without some merit. What Tirpitz and the Kaiser did not count on were three things. Firstly, the recall of the ships from the Far East, increasing Royal Navy strength in home waters. Secondly, the simple fact that Britain could out build Germany in dreadnoughts and thirdly the British reaction to the outbreak of war and the strategy employed which was quite simply to stand off and blockade Germany. Tirpitz and the Kaiser were expecting an immediate attack on its North Sea bases through heavily mined and submarine patrolled waters. It didn't happen. The Germans now had a choice. If they come out, they will be annihilated, if they stay in port Germany would starve. The Germans didn't know what to do.

Thus was the position in 1914 after war had broken out. The Royal Navy was based in Scapa Flow carrying out a standoff blockade of Germany whilst protecting its own sea lanes. The Germans now had to decide what to do. A vast amount of money had been spent on the navy and the people expected some return. The German fleet also wanted action however the Kaiser was loathed to risk his beloved ships. And so, the German Navy was to embark on the policy with a hit and run. The purpose of this strategy was for the Battle Cruiser Squadron (with the High Seas Fleet in support) to carry out raids on the seaside towns of England and draw out part of the Grand Fleet, probably the Battle Cruiser Fleet, and lead it into the guns of the main fleet and destroy it. Thus inflicting disproportionate attrition and wearing down the Grand Fleet. The initial attempts at this strategy were only partly successful in that seaside towns such as Scarborough were shelled but the Germans scurried away too quickly for the Royal Navy to catch them.

What the Germans were not aware of however was that the code breaking section known as Room 40 (based at the Admiralty in London) had cracked German codes and were aware of some of the movements. The Germans knew that there was a security problem somewhere, however they assumed incorrectly that intelligence was being gathered by the British fishing fleets off the Dogger Bank so in January 1915 the Battle Cruiser Squadron under Admiral Hipper swept into the Dogger Bank with a view to destroying the fishing vessels. The Royal Navy of course was tipped to this by Room 40 and the inconclusive battle of the Dogger Bank was fought with the result that the Germans were chased back to home waters having lost an armoured cruiser, the *Blucher.*

The battle was not terribly important as far as losses and tactical advantage was concerned, however it did highlight the difficulties of trying to control large amounts of warships in a battle. Flag signalling was still in use by the Royal Navy (little different from Nelson's time) only with the additional problems that a modern fleet gives, such as visual problems with thick acrid smoke in the air from guns and engines, higher speeds and of course greater distances. The German battle cruisers escaped because the British, not seeing the signals properly or misinterpreting them, concentrated their fire on one ship, the *Blucher*. This situation was also not helped by the Fleet Commander Admiral Beatty having to leave his flagship *HMS Lion* after she was hit. In the intervening time it took to move his command to a cruiser the battle had moved on and the battle cruisers rather than picking individual targets had instead concentrated their fire on the *Blucher*. The *Blucher* herself was not an important target, she was an armoured cruiser which was another experiment in warship design (pre-dreadnought) and she was in the Battle Cruiser Squadron simply because there was nowhere else to put her.

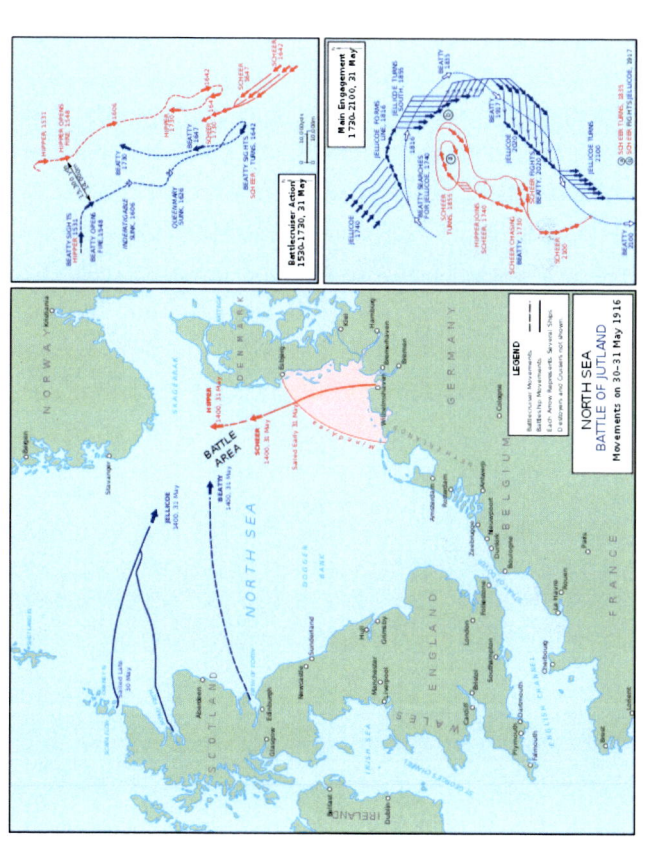

On the 30th May 1916 Room 40 intercepted intelligence which it understood to mean that the High Seas Fleet (or at least part of it, most likely the 1st Scouting Force) was preparing to leave harbour for a sortie into the North Sea. Jellicoe ordered the Grand Fleet and the Battle Cruiser Fleet (with the 5th Battle Squadron of the new fast *Queen Elizabeth* class battleships attached) to leave port with a view to joining up near Jutland and conducting a sweep. However, by midday on the 31st it was not clear which German units had left port. This was because the Admiralty had supposedly intercepted radio signals from Scheer's flagship which put her still in port. However, this was later identified as the code for the admiral when in port, not at sea, so the appearance later on of the High Seas Fleet would be as big a surprise to Jellicoe as the appearance of the Grand Fleet was to Scheer.

Admiral John Jellicoe

At 14.40 on the 31st May, the advance screening cruisers spotted smoke to the east and after investigating further *HMS Galatea* signalled to Beatty 'enemy in sight', it was Hipper's 1st Scouting Group. Beatty ordered a turn to the south, south, east in order to cut off Hipper and the opposing fleets began to converge. Here we see one of the poor command decisions of Beatty in that he opened fire at around the same time as Hipper when the bigger guns of his battle cruisers could in fact have opened fire earlier. At around 16.10 disaster struck for the first but not last time that day when the *Indefatigable* suddenly received hits from a salvo (probably fired by the *Von der Tann*) and promptly blew up. Only two seamen of the nine hundred crew survived. Disaster struck again at 16.26 when the combined fire of *Seydlitz* and *Derflinger* caused the *Queen Mary* to also explode killing all but twenty of her twelve hundred crew. This caused Beatty to make his famous remark to Ernle Chatfield, 'there seems to be something wrong with our bloody ships today!' There was. Not in the ships but in the handling of them in action. As noted earlier the Royal Navy was all about gunnery and rate of fire. This policy caused numerous mistakes to be made in the fire control of British warships, most notably: Flash doors were left open to make the passage of shells and cordite faster. Charges were left piled on deck ready for use. With all this together a hit on a turret (any turret) and the flame would pass right through to the magazine causing a massive explosion.

Admiral Reinhard Scheer

By this time the 5th Battle Squadron had now begun firing on the German battle cruisers when Admiral Goodenough in the light cruiser *Southampton* spotted the High Seas Fleet coming up from the south east, Beatty promptly turned north west in order to lead them onto the approaching Grand Fleet.

The battle now moved to the hopefully decisive phase of the two main battle fleets engaging. Jellicoe's first decision was to release Admiral Hood's 3rd Battle Cruiser Squadron to assist Beatty. Whilst this was underway Beatty withdrew from Hipper whose attention was turned to the 5th Battle Squadron. This squadron was still steaming south under Beatty's orders, no doubt surprised to pass his fleet moving the opposite way! Beatty had failed to relay his instructions to the squadron.

At 17.35 Beatty once more turned into the 1st Scouting Group in order to drive them off course away from the Grand Fleet, thus depriving Scheer of his eyes. At this time the 1st Scouting Group was also engaged by Hood's 3rd Battle Cruiser Squadron which had run into them by mistake. The resultant fighting ended in the loss of the German Light Cruiser, *Wiesbaden*. At 18.15 Jellicoe deployed his fleet from north west to east. This was probably the most important naval decision ever made in the Great War. Jellicoe was still uncertain as to the whereabouts of the High Seas Fleet. Beatty had still not given any indication of the course and speed of Scheer, most likely being too engrossed in his own battle and forgetting his primary purpose which was as a scouting group for the main fleet. Thus, Jellicoe had to make the most important decision of his career based on the last reports of Beatty's position and the sound of gunfire. It was the correct decision and allowed the Grand Fleet to cross the enemy's 'T'.

At 18.22 Scheer steamed right into any German admiral's worst nightmare, a one on one with the Grand Fleet with his 'T' crossed. Meanwhile Hipper sheared off pursued by Beatty and Hood. It was at this time that the third heavy loss of the day befell the Royal Navy when *Invincible* blew up in the same fashion as the previous two battle cruisers. For fifteen minutes the Grand Fleet pounded the leading battleships of the High Seas Fleet causing severe damage, yet not sinking a single battleship. This is a tribute to the design and construction of the German ships. Scheer then ordered a brilliant manoeuvre and all ships turned one hundred and ninety degrees and reversed course disappearing into the haze. However, twenty minutes later, Scheer ordered an about turn and headed back into the Grand Fleet. This order has caused much historical argument as it was an almost suicidal manoeuvre. The best guess is that Scheer was either hoping to cross the Grand Fleet's rear and cross its 'T' or most likely he was hoping to bypass the Grand Fleet entirely and sail around them back to Germany whilst Jellicoe looked to the Westward. In any event the only way out this time after another severe pounding was for Scheer to launch a mass torpedo attack from his destroyers whilst he turned the Battle Fleet away once again. This is where the historical debate really begins. Jellicoe's standing orders were quite clear in the event of a torpedo attack. The fleet will turn away. This is what he ordered thus allowing the Germans to escape. This was the end of the major fleet action. That night there was sporadic fighting as the fleets intermingled in the darkness. However, this action resulted in the loss of numerous destroyers and cruisers on either side as well as the elderly German pre-dreadnought *Pommern*. Again, communication was not forthcoming from the forces engaged and another opportunity to engage was missed.

HMS Southampton, last remaining Royal Navy ship from Jutland

The losses in the battle were heavy, certainly in lives lost. The British lost three battle cruisers, three armoured cruisers and nine destroyers along with around ten thousand men. German losses were one battle cruiser, one pre-dreadnought battleship, four cruisers and five destroyers with around two thousand five hundred men. Certainly tactically, the Germans had won the day by dint of killing more men and sinking more ships. However, battles (and certainly naval battles) are not judged on losses. They are judged on who commands the ground afterwards. In this respect the Royal Navy was victorious as it commanded the sea and continued its blockade of Germany. The Grand Fleet was ready for sea again twenty-four hours after returning to port, whereas the High Seas Fleet would not be able to put to sea again for some months due to the extreme damage inflicted on them in the encounter. Indeed, some ships would never put to sea again. It should also be noted that the Germans barely escaped and did so only due to the difficulties of controlling huge fleets at sea. When Tirpitz reported to the Kaiser after the battle he said, "We must never do this again, we will be destroyed."

Historians and leading figures after the battle have all attempted to dissect the engagement and apportion blame for the failure of the Royal Navy to make a better showing of itself. Some (including Beatty) have sought to change history and make Jellicoe the scapegoat for what was considered a rather mediocre performance of the Grand Fleet. Others have sought to lionise Jellicoe for his masterly handling of what was a very difficult set piece battle. I am of the latter school of thought and I will give my reasons why.

1. The job of the battle cruiser as conceived was not to take position in the line of battle, it was to act as the eyes of the main fleet and report enemy course and speed. Of course Beatty engaged Hipper in the best traditions of the Royal Navy, however he failed to report in full the movements of the High Seas Fleet to Jellicoe, thus leaving him to make an educated guess as to its course and speed. Beatty also failed to include the 5th Battle Squadron (which was attached to his command) in his orders and movements. This not only deprived him of five of the most powerful and advanced battleships in the world, it also caused them to run into enemy forces at a disadvantage.
2. Jellicoe's decision to deploy during the battle was perhaps the most important and bravest order ever given in a sea battle, comparable to Nimitz's decision to sortie at Midway twenty-five years later. Without the intelligence of Beatty he judged through experience and knowledge of the sea when and where to deploy. Had he been wrong the Germans would have crossed his 'T' to his rear causing huge damage. One must put oneself in Jellicoe's shoes and realise that he was the only man who

could lose the war in a single battle. The most controversial order of the day was for the fleet to turn away from the torpedo attack. Again, the right decision. This was criticised by Beatty after the battle, however it should be remembered that Beatty did exactly the same thing at the Dogger Bank a year earlier. Torpedoes had proved to be devastating weapons and could well have severely damaged or sunk a dozen battleships. The object of the battle was not to destroy the enemy but to keep the seas and force the Germans back to port.

The Battle of Jutland was not of course the only naval battle of WWI, but alongside the vital defence of the trade routes over the North Atlantic it was the most important. Whereas the victory over the German submarine arm was essential to Britain's survival, equally the holding at bay and neutralising of the German surface fleet was vital to Germany's defeat.

Historians now, in light of the centenary celebrations especially, are looking at this battle in more detail and especially its part in the winning of the war. Modern technology has allowed historians and archaeologists to investigate the ships sunk and the damage done adding more evidence to the already known effects of poor handling of munitions and the rapid-fire doctrine, of the Royal Navy at that time. For my part to reiterate my earlier thoughts I would go so far as to say that this battle was instrumental in the defeat of Germany. Of course the final offensives of 1918 on the western front broke the back of the German Army but it was a German Army that was starving and what little food Germany had was taken from the civilian population in Germany, this in itself caused low morale in the army as soldiers worried about their families back home.

The Battle of Jutland could well have cost Britain the war had she not retained possession of the seas. Equally it caused the defeat of Germany through old fashioned blockade which in the 20th century was just as potent a weapon as it had ever been.

Norway 1940

I have included this naval conflict in my narrative for three reasons. Firstly, it was a classic use of sea power by both sides, on the German side in order to facilitate invasion and on the Royal Navy side an expedition to land an army and stop an enemy from landing his. Secondly, it was a naval gun battle, as the second world war progressed the use of airpower was making ship to ship action more redundant. Thirdly and most importantly I firmly believe that the naval battles over Norway were instrumental in having a direct influence on the conduct of the war for the remainder of World

War II. We see the removal of key units of the German Navy from operations for the foreseeable future, thus relaxing the strain on convoys. We also see a diminution of the number of German destroyers and cruisers which would have been crucial to any later successful landing in Britain, despite air superiority. The battles over Norway reduced the German surface fleet by two battle cruisers, three cruisers and ten destroyers either sunk or out of action. These craft would have been vital in the confined waters of the English Channel and would have provided both escort for the invasion barges as well as close in-shore fire support.

If Germany had achieved air superiority over the RAF during the Battle of Britain they would still have had to try and bomb Royal Navy ships which would not have been an easy task. Granted, Royal Navy and French Navy destroyers were sunk at Dunkirk during the evacuation of allied troops but these were often tied up on jetties or operating in the confines of the harbour, consider them trying to attack much faster and more manoeuvrable destroyers and cruisers with anti-aircraft armament and far more ability to conduct damage control. I pose the question that even if the Luftwaffe had been victorious and knocked out the RAF would an invasion have been a very risky proposal without a surface fleet to both protect it and provide fire support? It is of course pure conjecture but I would ask the reader to consider the vast armada that the Allies used in the Normandy invasion of 1944. There was virtually no threat from the German Navy at that time but we do see small numbers of fast attack craft causing problems during the invasion despite the massive allied escorting fleet and indeed one allied destroyer was sunk by surface craft on D-Day. In any event I include this epic naval story in my narrative for all the reasons above, other historians may well disagree but I think it certainly merits the question.

The shipments of iron ore supplies to Germany from Sweden through Narvik were of major concern to the British Government and First Lord of the Admiralty, Winston Churchill was especially irked that the Royal Navy was not able to stop the shipments as they were in neutral waters. In February 1940 the Royal Navy destroyer, *Cossack* successfully intercepted and boarded the German supply ship *Altmark* in a Norwegian fjord. This was done in flagrant disregard of Norwegian neutrality but was justified by the British because the *Altmark* contained over four hundred British seamen captured during the rampage of the *Graf Spee* in 1939. In fairness the British undertook the operation because the Norwegian authorities only half-heartedly stopped and searched the *Altmark* and did not find the sailors on board. This sent a clear message to the Allied powers that Norwegian neutrality was going to be ignored by the Germans, therefore they needed to do something to deny that long stretch of coast to the German Navy.

Churchill had the idea of mining Norwegian waters to intercept the iron ore traffic. After some discussion within the British War Cabinet this was finally agreed and set for the 8th April. Across the sea the Germans were having much the same discussion about Norwegian neutrality. After all a British warship had entered Norwegian waters and stormed a German ship whilst the Norwegian authorities stood by and did nothing. However, their response went far further than a deployment of mines, Hitler planned for an invasion of Norway.

On 9th April, the German invasion of Norway began with an assault on Denmark. This small virtually defenceless country was overrun in less than a day. At the same time German troops under General Falkenhorst were landing at Oslo, Bergen, Trondheim and Narvik. In conjunction with this German paratroops landed and seized Sola airport near Stavanger and Fornebu airport near Oslo.

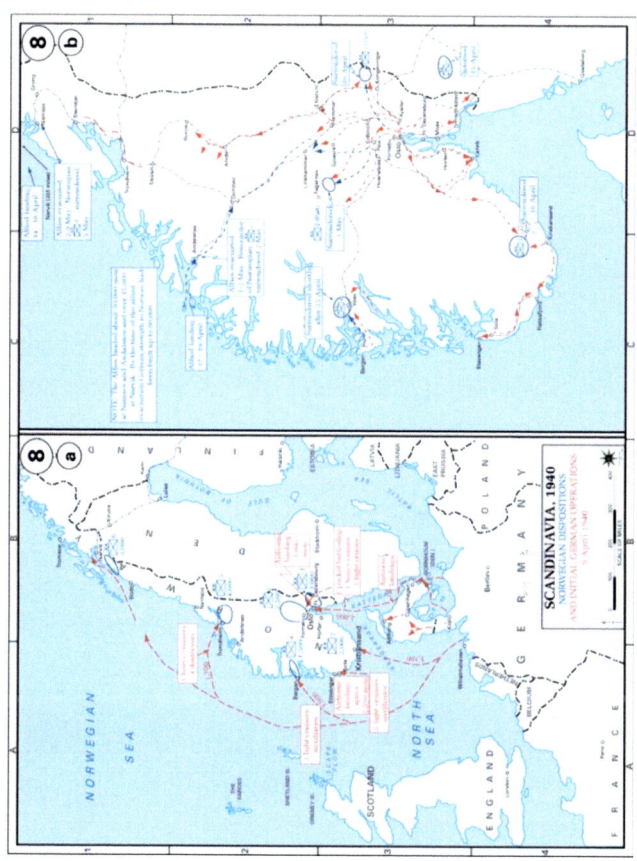

On this day we also saw the first German naval losses of the campaign. Firstly, the new German heavy cruiser *Blucher* was sunk by Norwegian coastal defences and the light cruiser *Karlsruhe* sunk by the submarine *HMS Truant*. The *Blucher* was the flagship of Admiral Kumnetz of Marine Group 5 which consisted of the heavy cruiser *Blucher*, the heavy cruiser (or pocket battleship) *Lutzow*, the light cruise *Emden* three torpedo boats and eight minesweepers. The *Karlsruhe* was in the process of landing troops at Kristiansand with an E-boat tender, four E-boats and several torpedo boats. Also, on 9th April, the heavy cruiser, *Hipper* was rammed by the destroyer, *HMS Gloworm* gouging a one-hundred-and-twenty-foot hole in her starboard bow and earning the first posthumous VC of the campaign for her captain, Lt Commander Roope. A satisfactory day for the Royal Navy all told, however German troops were landed and beginning operations to conquer the country.

On 10th April, the Royal Navy counter attacked by sending the 2nd Destroyer Flotilla of five H-class destroyers into Narvik where they engaged and sank two German destroyers and damaged three others. They also sank six German merchant ships, all without loss. However, on their return journey through the fjords out of Narvik they were engaged by six German destroyers and lost two destroyers sunk and one damaged. The German destroyers suffered some damage and the merchant ship *Raunfels* was sunk. The flotilla commander, Commodore Warburton Lee was also killed and was awarded the second posthumous VC for the Royal Navy.

The victorious German destroyers continued their journey in to Narvik where on the 13th April Vice Admiral Whitworth flying his flag in the Queen Elisabeth class battleship, *HMS Warspite* with nine destroyers engaged and sank eight German destroyers. During the same engagement the sea plane from *Warspite* sunk a German U-boat, the first ever sinking in history by a naval aircraft.

This saw the end of major naval engagements over Norway until 7th June, when the carrier, *HMS Glorious* and her two escorting destroyers were sunk by the German battle cruisers, *Scharnhorst* and *Gneisenau* however both these ships were damaged and put out of action for the rest of the year.

In terms of losses the Royal Navy was certainly the winner with only five destroyers and one carrier sunk. The German Navy lost ten destroyers, two cruisers, one U-boat and crucially two battle cruisers and one heavy cruiser badly damaged. The real victor however was Germany. Hitler had audaciously landed an army in Norway in the teeth of the Royal Navy, quickly overcome the weak Norwegian Army and put the conquering German troops into a strong position in which to repel any intervention by the Allies. British and French troops were landed but proved to be woefully inadequate in fighting both the hostile climate and terrain and against a dominant Luftwaffe and were eventually withdrawn. Despite the Royal Navy tactical victories strategically this was an allied defeat and one which would have dire consequences on the remainder of the war. German naval and air units were able to operate out of Norway against the convoys to Russia doing much damage to British and allied merchant shipping and tying down Royal Navy units to defend against German capital ships such as *Tirpitz, Scharnhorst* and *Gneisenau.* On the plus side for the Allies though the defeat led to the downfall of the Chamberlain government in early May 1940, a positive act which prevented a British capitulation early in the war. The conquest of Norway also had benefits for the Allies in that it tied down twelve German divisions which Hitler insisted on keeping in Norway in case the Allies chose to launch their second front there. This constituted over five percent of the German Army in 1944 which could have been used to more effect in Russia but in fact played no further part in war.

Going back to my earlier points this removed from future German naval operations fifty percent of her entire destroyer force and several key heavy units. Thus, making in my humble opinion an invasion of Britain later in the year virtually impossible despite possible mastery of the air. The battle was lost by the Allies but with the exception of a few capital ships the threat of the German surface fleet had been removed from the northern theatre of operations.

I firmly believe that for all reasons stated above, both political and military we can draw a direct line from the campaign in Norway, right the way to the end of the war in the west; this is why I have included it in this book.

Midway 1942

Japanese carrier Hiryu ablaze

I have always considered this one of the most important naval battles of the second world war. Had the United States Navy lost this battle and their three remaining Carriers the whole of the west coast of America would have been open to attack. The American victory meant that the Japanese were now to be on the defensive and lose the initiative in the Pacific war.

From the time that war broke out in December 1941, Admiral Yamamoto the Commander in Chief of the Japanese Imperial Navy, had major concerns about a long, protracted war with the United States. Yamamoto was very familiar with America having been the Naval Attaché there and knew the power and resources of the nation. In contrast, Japan had few resources of her own, hence her campaign to create an empire in the far east. He understood that a highly successful pre-emptive strike against the US Navy Pacific Fleet based at Pearl Harbour in Hawaii was the only way to achieve anything like a supremacy against such a huge industrial nation like the United States. This he hoped would give time for Japan to extend her empire to include the valuable resource rich regions of South East Asia, fortify the gains then sit back and wait for the inevitable counter strike which hopefully could be contained. There was even the possibility that if the US fleet was knocked out straight away the United States may well sue for peace. As Yamamoto put it to the Japanese Government and high command Japan could wreak havoc for six months maybe twelve. The Achilles heel of Japan was lack of oil. Right up to the end of the war oil was shipped to Japan and her conquered territories and as a consequence much was lost to US submarines. In late 1941 the oil situation was becoming critical due to America's embargo in response to Japan's aggressive war in China. Diplomatic missions were taking place but these paid lip service only to finding a solution to the deadlock so in late November the code words 'Climb Mount Niitaka' were sent out to the Japanese Imperial Navy and the attack on Pearl Harbour was to proceed. Stores of oil allowed only a few months more of operations so time had run out for the ever less likely successful conclusion to the talks.

The Japanese Imperial Navy at this time was very committed to aircraft carriers, they saw the potential of these fighting units and even though they were equally committed to large battleships it was the inability to produce them that forced them down the path of carriers. We have to go back to the aftermath of WWI for the origins of modern battlefleets and in particular to the Washington Treaty of 1922.

The Washington Treaty was quite simply designed to prevent another war. After World War I and the scuttling of the German fleet the US and British Governments began looking around for the next enemy and the next potential war to fight. It was believed in some quarters that trade caused wars so the US Navy, bizarrely it now seems, began planning for war with Britain. Britain for her part could not continue to build battleships at the rate previously seen before the war so when the United States suggested a treaty to limit warships it was greeted eagerly.

Essentially the Washington Treaty concentrated on amounts in numbers, tonnage and calibre of guns. Cruisers were limited to ten thousand tons, battleships to thirty-five thousand tons and sixteen inch guns. Carriers were included in the treaty being limited to twenty-seven thousand tons but signatories were allowed to both use existing hulls of capital ships and class several of their carriers as experimental and not subject to the treaty limitations. We also see the magic 5-5-3 ratio whereby the US and Britain would have parity in battleship numbers but the rising navies of the world including Japan would be limited to three for every five British and American battleships. This put Japan at a major disadvantage if war came against either or both the US and Britain, another way to secure naval power had to be found and this way was the aircraft carrier.

Aircraft carriers were not a new invention, there had been a seaplane carrier with the Grand Fleet at Jutland and indeed a large air raid was planned for 1919 by the Royal Navy on the German High Seas Fleet at anchor so naval air warfare was nothing new. What was new and what had not happened as yet was the sinking of a battleship by aircraft.

General Billy Mitchell of the US Army was a staunch believer in airpower trumping all other military doctrines including naval power. His experiments in the 1920s were to show that battleships could be sunk by aircraft and this was proved when an old German dreadnought the *Ostfriesland* was sunk by Mitchell's squadrons. However, was this decisive evidence? Most navies thought not. Yes, a battleship had been sunk but it took far more bombs than were originally thought and far longer. Indeed, Mitchell carried out his initial attack in the time allotted but not being successful he simply carried on until the ship was sunk. The naval thinkers at the time simply said okay, you sank a battleship that had no crew, was dead in the water, had no anti-aircraft armament and no damage control, big deal, it proved nothing in their eyes. Aircraft carriers had a use certainly as did aircraft but the use was in scouting, anti-submarine work and assisting the surface fleet. Battleships were still the way forward in most navies' minds except the Japanese Navy who though heavily committed to battleships considered them to be the final arbiters of victory in a sea battle rather than a central element.

Japan was building battleships but had to cease with the signing of the Washington Treaty and this left ships' hulls that could be easily converted to carry flight decks and this is exactly what the Japanese Navy did and as a consequence at the start of war with the United States in 1941 Japan had eight carriers to America's four in the Pacific, a decisive ratio. The Japanese Naval Air arm was equally important, highly trained and considered an elite force.

The plan for an airborne attack on Pearl Harbour had been considered by both the US Navy and the Japanese Navy. The one act that caused the Japanese Navy to look further at this was the Royal Navy raid on Taranto in November 1940 where a dozen old Swordfish bi-planes were able to sink or put out of action several Italian battleships at anchor in Taranto harbour. If planes could get through, they could sink large warships. Pearl harbour however differed from Taranto in that it is a shallow harbour with a depth of about forty feet, too shallow for an air launched torpedo which needed more depth to bottom out and level off at just below sea level. Japanese scientists solved this problem by attaching fins to the torpedoes to lessen the rate of descent in water, an attack could now go ahead.

On 7th December 1941, early in the morning, the first waves of Japanese aircraft swept in and attacked the US battlefleet at anchor. Eighteen ships were sunk or damaged including the nucleus of the Pacific Fleet at that time, five battleships. Aircraft were also destroyed along with port facilities however two vital targets escaped the attack, the vast oil containers and above all the US Navy carriers which were out delivering aircraft to Wake and Midway islands. Yamamoto was thrilled with the success of the raid but conscious of the fact that the carriers had escaped.

As Yamamoto had predicted the Japanese Navy ran riot for six months in a series of decisive naval confrontations and invasions. On 10th December, the pride of the Royal Navy in the Far East sent to deter Japanese aggression the battleship, *Prince of Wales* and the old battlecruiser, *Repulse* were sunk off the coast of Malaya and in so doing became the first battleships at sea to be sunk by aircraft. This was swiftly followed up by the Battle of the Java Sea in which several ABDA (American, Dutch, British and Australian) cruisers and destroyers were sunk. The Japanese Indian Ocean raid then drove the Royal Navy out of the Pacific and over to the East African coast. The Pacific was open to the Japanese Navy. But what now? There were still four US Navy carriers in the Pacific and these were about to show their strength and range with the famous Doolittle Raid of 18th April 1942. B25 bombers taking off from the US carriers, *Hornet* and *Enterprise* bombed Tokyo doing very little damage but sending the signal that Japan was not out of reach and most important of all to the Japanese the Emperor was not safe. The carriers had to be dealt with.

Yamamoto knew that the destruction of the US Navy was imperative to Japan's war aims but the loss of the battleships was not as much of a disaster as one first thinks. Fleet carriers are faster and fight their battles from a distance, keeping battleships at bay. In fact, battleships at this time were in the throws of being relegated to a secondary role of anti-aircraft support, shore bombardment and as insurance against surface attack. In fact at the time of the Pearl Harbour raid Admiral Halsey declined the offer of the battleships to accompany his carriers with the delivery of aircraft to Wake and Midway as they would slow him down. Yamamoto now had to consider how to destroy the US Navy carrier fleet, thus operation MI was conceived.

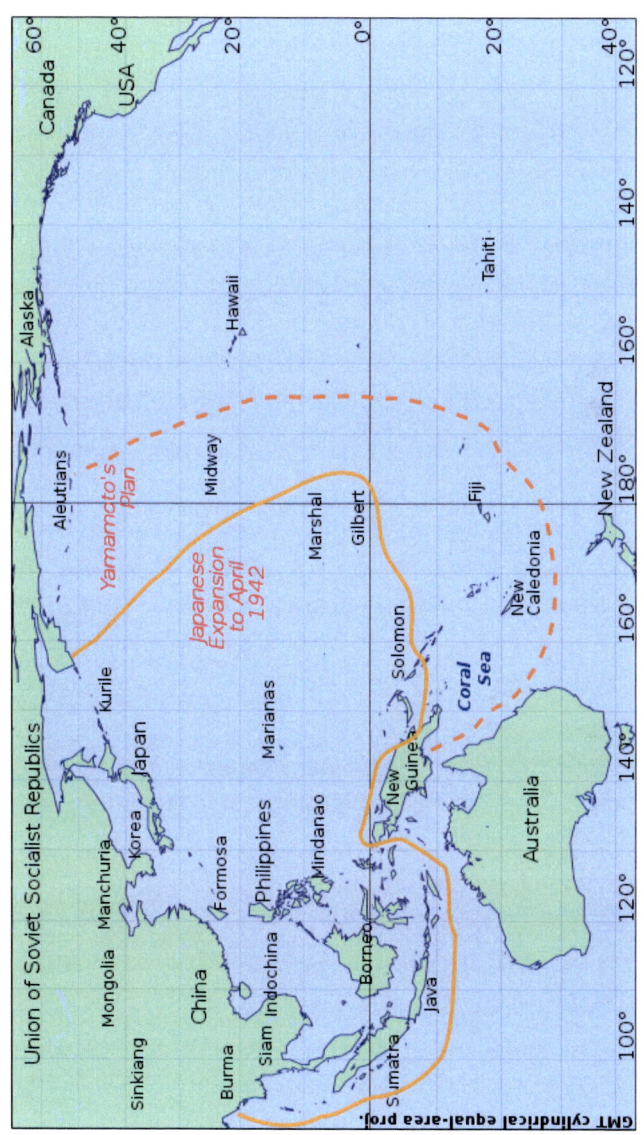

Japanese expansion to April 1942

Operation MI was quite simply an elaborate trap to entice out the US Navy's carrier force. The plan was bold and simple in its conception, but unnecessarily complicated in its execution. The plan was to launch an invasion of the Aleutian Islands as a prelude and diversion to the invasion of Midway Island. The plan then hinged on wrong footing the Americans and forcing them to react to the attack on Midway and go blindly into the entire Imperial Japanese Navy and subsequent annihilation. The US fleet would leave Pearl Harbour and head for Midway, along the route would be a line of submarines which would pick off key ships and any that got to Midway would be destroyed by aircraft of the Japanese 1st Carrier Fleet under Vice Admiral Nagumo. Any mopping up would be done by the main battle fleet led by Yamamoto himself in his flagship the seventy thousand ton, eighteen inch gunned *Yamato,* the largest battleship in the world.

However, this complicated plan was to presuppose that the Americans would do all that Japan intended, they did not.

American Naval Intelligence had cracked the Japanese Navy's code which uncovered the MI plan but not the target which was designated in code as AF, at this stage MI was meaningless. Then after back tracking Japanese radio signal intercepts it looked highly possible that AF could be Midway Island. An intelligence plot was hatched to test this theory and a message was sent from Midway to Hawaii telling of a fresh water condenser fault on the island. As anticipated this was intercepted and sent by code to Japanese Naval Headquarters from a listening post at Kwajalein with the statement that AF had a water condenser issue. AF had to be Midway, now the US Navy could move.

We need here to backtrack slightly and incorporate into this narrative the Battle of the Coral Sea. Quite a significant battle in that it stopped part of a Japanese invasion of New Guinea forcing the army to traverse the Owen Stanley Range of mountains at great cost. However, for this narrative the sea battle has an added importance as the Japanese sunk the US carrier, *Saratoga* and so badly damaged the carrier, *Yorktown* that it was reported to have been sunk. At the time this was not denied by the US Navy as they were hoping to limp her home which they managed, *Yorktown* docking only hours before the main group set off for Midway.

Now that the invasion of Midway Island with the all-crucial dates had been ascertained, the US carriers of Task Force 16 set sail for Midway three days before they were expected to by the Japanese, thus avoiding the line of submarines. Task Force 16 under the newly promoted Admiral Ray Spruance contained at its core the carriers, *Enterprise* and *Hornet* with supporting cruisers and destroyers. Admiral Jack Fletcher's *Yorktown* which had been miraculously repaired in forty-eight hours set sail a matter of hours later with the intention of rendezvousing with Spruance at a point north east of Midway to lie in wait for the Japanese.

USS Yorktown at Pearl Harbour, May 1942

With the Japanese fleet now at sea and heading for Midway and the Aleutians it was still believed that the US carriers were at Hawaii. A plan had been conceived where long range sea planes would fly over Pearl Harbour and report if the carriers were still there. However due to a US Navy vessel being at French Frigate Shoals, the planned point for a refuel of the planes, they were unable to replenish from the submarine waiting there and continue on to Pearl Harbour so the reconnaissance was cancelled. This was not transmitted to the fleet as it would have meant breaking radio silence which meant that they had to go on existing intelligence, intelligence that put the carriers at Pearl Harbour with no reason to have left.

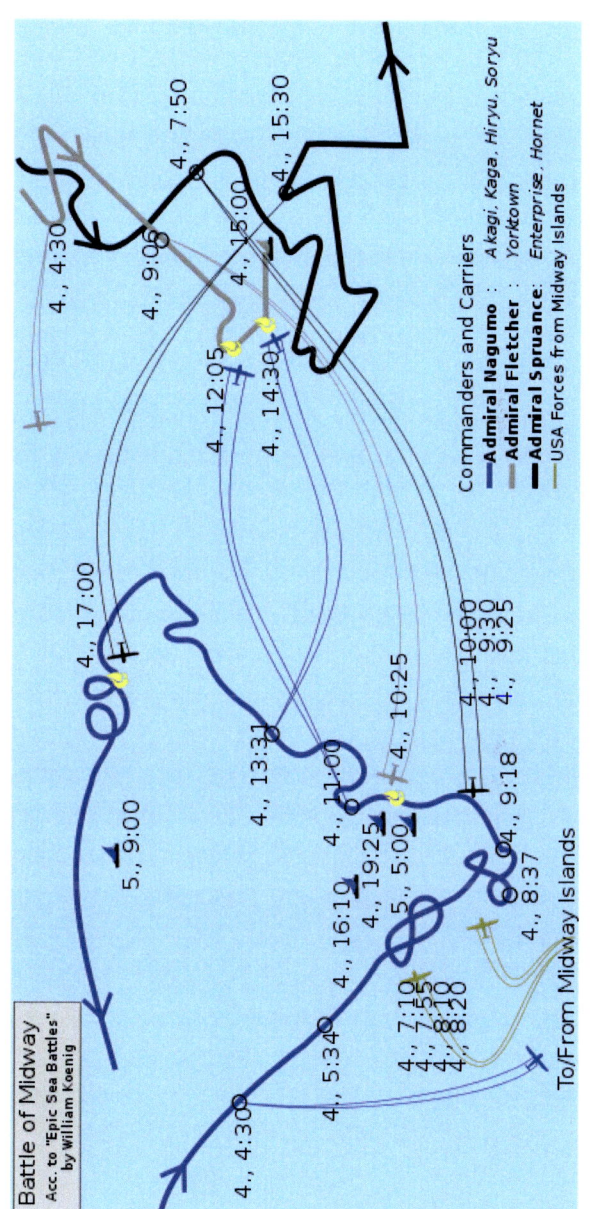

The battle opened on the 5th June with the Japanese carrier force launching an attack on Midway Island's airfield. This attack was valiantly met by fighters of the US Marine Corps, however the Japanese aircraft breezed right through them, the old Brewster Buffalos being no match for the A6M Zero. They then proceeded to bomb the airfield. An attack had already been launched by the aircraft on Midway and ten torpedo bombers attacked the Japanese carriers but without result and one hundred percent casualties. This was followed by attacks from Fortress bombers with again no effect.

The elated Japanese aircrew returned to their home carriers with tales of direct hits and much damage done, however the airfield was still in working order. This left Vice Admiral Nagumo with a stark choice. Should a follow up attack be launched or should the aircraft quickly re-arm to repel any possible naval attack by the US Navy. No sightings had been reported by Nagumo's scout planes who were searching for the US Navy, however the cruiser, *Tone* had experienced catapult problems so its scout plane was thirty minutes late taking off.

Having received no confirmation that the carriers were at Pearl Harbour Nagumo, a very cautious man, was now torn between a second strike on Midway or a strike posture against any US carriers in the area. Being unaware of any US ships and knowing that Midway still posed a threat with its airfield in operation he opted for the former and ordered a second strike on Midway. Events then moved rapidly as the scout plane from the *Tone* reported 'enemy in sight' having sighted ten enemy ships to the north east, Spruance's Task Force 16.

Nagumo immediately ordered a reversal of the attack on Midway and had his aircraft's bombs replaced with torpedoes, a lengthy and costly action as events would prove. Meanwhile 116 US Navy aircraft from Task Force 16 were about to attack Nagumo's Carrier Fleet. Torpedo planes came in first having risked going into the attack with no fighter cover which had got lost on the way. All twenty-nine US torpedo bombers were shot down without any hits to the carriers, an appalling loss. However, they did achieve a vitally important consequence which was to bring the Japanese fighter cover down to sea level and draw them off from the carriers as the fighter pilots could not resist wave hopping after the bombers. This meant no top fighter cover for the carrier group, a major tactical disadvantage. At ten a.m. the Japanese carriers were still changing ordnance and with their decks crowded with aircraft and discarded bombs from the ill-fated change over, US Navy dive bombers led by Lt Commander Max Leslie and Lt Commander Wade McClusky carried out the most devastating aerial attack against warships in the history of warfare and hit three carriers simultaneously, *Akagi, Kaga* and *Soryu* all of which caught fire and later sank.

Japanese carrier Akagi

The attack was a devastating success but the battle was not yet over. The fourth Japanese carrier, *Hyryu* was untouched and immediately launched a counter attack against the only US carrier that had been reported, the *Yorktown*. After successive attacks the Yorktown was reported to be ablaze and sinking however, she survived until the following day when she finally sunk. At this stage of the battle with a ratio of three to one any other commander may have ordered

Task Force 16 home but the new C in C Pacific Admiral Chester Nimitz wanted the fourth carrier and so ordered Task Force 16 to find and sink the *Hyryu* which they did, setting her ablaze just like her ill-fated sisters of the 1st Carrier Fleet. Yamamoto decided enough was enough and withdrew leaving a heavy cruiser squadron as rear guard which was attacked the next day and the heavy cruiser, *Mogami* sunk. This marked the end of the battle.

Thus ended, in my opinion, the most decisive naval battle in modern times, from now on Japan knew that the writing was on the wall. The US Navy now had the initiative and Japan was forced to fall back on her defensive ring of islands, never again launching a naval attack with any hope of success. Also due to the attack on Pearl Harbour in December 1941, a negotiable peace was out of the question.

The Falklands 1982

HMS Invicible returning to Portsmouth after the Falklands War, 1982

The routes of the Falklands War go back to the age-old disputes of territory ownership. Argentina is quite a young country but has always claimed ownership of the islands. However due to the fact that Great Britain is a maritime power and had up to the end of the second world war the largest empire in history, outlying islands such as the Falklands were of immense importance to her communications. With the advent of steam powered warships the Falklands along with many other islands worldwide became in effect coaling and telegraph stations and areas where ships could lay up and repair. Needless to say to a maritime nation these are of huge importance. Alongside the strategic importance these islands in their turn attract settlers from the mother country, so eventually after many years you have inhabitants who are British and wish to remain so.

Throughout the 1960s and 70s negotiations with Argentina over the sovereignty of the islands were progressing and a possible solution may have been found but for the inhabitants who wished to remain British, and would not countenance becoming part of Argentina. Their case was further strengthened by the appalling human rights record of Argentina. The political fallout of giving away these people to a regime such as Argentina would have been huge and so the negotiations continued without progress until 1981 when events began to take a different turn.

General Leopoldo Galtieri took control of Argentina in 1981 leading a military junta to govern the country. The economy was at rock bottom and the popularity of the junta no better so Galtieri was forced to take drastic measures, one of which was a gamble to liberate the Malvinas (Falkland Islands). This would prove very popular with the public and take away some of the flak from the poor economic performance of the nation. National prestige would make the junta more credible. Ironically this is one of the reasons why the British Government also reacted so pugnaciously. Indeed, the

Falklands war cannot be underestimated in giving Mrs Thatcher and the Conservative Party in Britain their second term in office. Of course this was considered a gamble by Galtieri but quite a calculated and clever one in that he was sure that Britain would not react. Galtieri based his gamble on the following beliefs:

1. Britain had its own economic problems. The MoD was overseeing a shrinking budget and a large diminution of our military strength. Inevitably it was the Navy that was targeted most heavily.
2. The passing of the British Nationality Act in 1981. This legislation was designed to limit immigration to the UK of former colonial states and countries. It was aimed primarily at Hong Kong and limited immigration to people who could claim at least one grandparent from the UK. Gibraltar was exempted from this and attempts were made to exempt the Falkland Islands as well. However, these attempts proved unsuccessful. This was taken by Argentina as another clear indication that Britain would not support the islanders.
3. The Royal Navy was withdrawing its only presence in the South Atlantic, the ice patrol ship Endurance (with her tiny complement of Royal Marines). Galtieri read this as a clear indication that Britain had no concern for the area.

4. The assumption that militarily the Royal Navy was not equipped to mount an operation to recapture the islands even if she wanted to and regardless of the MoD's economic situation. Certainly on paper, this assumption has merit.

This fourth point bears much consideration and I do think that Galtieri had a point. The Royal Navy was heavily committed to NATO and her fleet consisted of destroyers and frigates in the main with only one aircraft carrier *Hermes* (*Invincible* was about to be sold to Australia but this was immediately cancelled so that she could join the task force) and a small landing ship squadron for 3 Commando Brigade. Not a particularly large force for retaking islands from a hostile power outside of the range of air cover and three thousand miles from the nearest base with poor weather closing in.

However, Galtieri did not count on four things. Firstly, the iron will of the British Prime Minister Mrs Thatcher who was eager to regain the Falklands either through peace or war. One must always remember that the putting together of a task force to recapture the islands was primarily a diplomatic lever, certainly until it reached the islands.

Secondly the Admiral of the Fleet Sir Henry Leach realised that an operation of this kind would deliver a *fete accompli* to the government over defence cuts. It would allow him to keep his carriers and the Royal

Marines moving forward. However, this was not a military gamble on his part. He consulted his colleagues and they agreed with him that such an operation was feasible out of the range of air cover due to the Sea Dart anti-aircraft missile system now employed on some Royal Navy destroyers and the Sea Wolf deployed on frigates. These systems provided between them far out and close in anti-aircraft and anti-missile defence and of course the land element of 3 Commando Brigade was sure that if landed safely they could retake the islands by force. The Royal Marines Commando specialised in fighting in inhospitable climates. They trained on Dartmoor and took a lead role along with the Royal Netherland Marine Commandos in the defence of Norway in the event of a Soviet attack.

Royal Navy Hawker Sea Harriers

Thirdly and quite simply was sea harrier. An ideal dog fighter which carried the all-important American Sidewinder heat seeking air to air missile. The air war was to prove a vital element to the campaign, however as the story unfolds it will be seen that though Britain did not lose the air war, she did not win it either. As a consequence, the troops had to land on a hostile shore without air superiority, not a good tactic, however feasible with the landing area chosen and the poor quality of the Argentine land forces deployed. In any event the British had to either make a landing very soon or withdraw before the severe winter weather began.

Fourth and last, naval interdiction. As soon as Britain was able, she deployed nuclear SSK submarines to the area effectively sealing off the Falklands from Argentina. This meant that supplies had to be flown in which both limited the amounts delivered and brought the supply planes under threat from the sea harriers and roaming warships as the task force drew near. Port Stanley airfield was also constantly shelled by task force ships limiting the capability of the airfield and disrupting the ingress and egress of supply planes.

With the advent of NATO and the shrinking of the empire after WWII the Royal Navy entered a period of decline which has never ceased to this day. The NATO alliance provided Britain with a completely different strategic role in that it became the guardians of the sea lanes between Europe and North America. The Royal Navy became in essence an anti-submarine force with no vessel larger than a destroyer for offensive action and indeed only through-deck cruisers (aircraft carriers) with very limited aircraft capability. The through-deck cruisers were designed as a response to the scrapping of the larger aircraft carriers which were decommissioned in the late 1970s. The government of the time considered that the priority for the Royal Navy was the NATO commitment and in anti-submarine role carriers were not required. However, the Admiralty was not happy with this and saw a real threat to the service in removing an air capability. Should the Fleet Air Arm lose its fighter and ground attack capability then there would be no role for the Royal Marines Commando, as they could not be expected to launch seaborne landings without air cover. This would have brought the RMC under army control and reduce them to infantry operating on NATO's northern flank. The Admiralty was foxed. However, during the 1960s a rather remarkable aircraft was designed, the Hawker Harrier. The Royal Navy realised that this could be flown off of a considerably smaller carrier due to its short take off capability and its VSTOL landing. Thus, a new breed of warship was envisaged and classed as the through-deck cruiser or anti-submarine cruiser. The Admiralty sold this to the government as a cruiser with the capability of launching helicopters for anti-submarine duties, however rather craftily they never showed the flight deck as this would have given the game away. In order to assist in the concealment of the fixed wing aircraft element further the ships were given traditional cruiser names, *Invincible* and *Illustrious*. Once these were launched however the navy could name the last of the class *Ark Royal*, a traditional carrier name. However, carriers or not, the *Invincible* and the older WWII veteran *Hermes* could only carry fifteen Harriers between them, not a huge amount compared to Argentina's two hundred or so combat aircraft. Also, with the loss of the fleet carriers there were no Gannet electronic surveillance aircraft for early warning cover of the fleet so standing patrols had to be used, thus making maintenance of the harriers a difficulty. However, the Fleet Air Arm harriers, performed magnificently shooting down over twenty enemy aircraft without loss in air-to-air combat. Sadly, there just weren't enough of them to cover both the Fleet and the landings and subsequent land campaign, thus the landings took place without full air cover, a huge risk.

The Royal Navy task force assembled for Operation Corporate was a formidable one, it needed to be. The force was to operate over eight thousand miles away with no port or dry dock facilities in some of the worst weather conditions in the world. The force would consist of two carriers, six submarines, eight destroyers, fifteen frigates and twenty-one RFA ships as well as the landing craft and landing ships for 3 Commando Brigade. This force was further augmented by STUFT (ships taken up from trade) a tradition dating back centuries.

The only rapid deployment force available for use straight away was 3 Commando Brigade Royal Marines. However, three Royal Marine Commandos of battalion strength were clearly not enough to wrest control of the islands from over ten thousand Argentine troops regardless of their quality. Therefore, the brigade needed to be reinforced and the most mobile element of the army's rapid deployment force 5 Infantry Brigade was allocated to 3 Commando Brigade. Fortunately, these were the two toughest and best trained Infantry battalions in the British Army, 2nd and 3rd Battalions of the Parachute Regiment. To follow would be the remaining element of 5 Brigade, the 7th Gurkha Rifles. To supplement 5 Infantry Brigade and bring it up to strength was a different matter. Due to the defence cuts and the commitment to the British Army of the Rhine there were very few up to strength regiments that could be called upon with such immediacy. The only brigade in the UK at anything like standby was the infantry element of the Household Division, the famous Guards regiments. Therefore, the Welsh and Scots Guards were ordered to join 5 Brigade and proceed south.

HMS Broadsword and HMS Hermes

To accompany the brigades there were numerous other army elements. These included the renowned 22 Regiment Special Air Service, The Royal Engineers, a troop from the Blues and Royals with eight light tanks and the Royal Army Medical Corps. These were complemented by Royal Marine elements of the Special Boat Squadron and 29 Regiment Royal Artillery the Royal Marine's artillery accompaniment. There were also Blowpipe and Rapier batteries for anti-aircraft defence.

Even before official confirmation that the islands had been captured Operation Corporate was ordered and the Royal Navy began assembling its resources. The nearest assets were the Royal Navy First Flotilla under

Rear Admiral Woodward engaged on Exercise Spring Train in the mid-Atlantic. These were ordered south to Ascension Island and consisted of the two large county class destroyers *Antrim* and *Glamorgan* along with the Type 42 Air Defence destroyers, *Sheffield, Glasgow, and Coventry*. There were also two frigates, *Brilliant and Arrow*.

The vital core of the naval force was to be the two carriers *Hermes* and *Invincible* with their complements of Fleet Air Arm sea harriers and helicopters, these assets set sail on the 5th April from Portsmouth amid much media hype, calculated to assist the diplomatic turning of the screw which was still the main effort to secure a peaceful outcome. As a prelude to the capture of the islands and again as a diplomatic lever a small force of ships designated Task Force 317.9 were to be dispatched to re-take South Georgia which had also been taken by the Argentines. This consisted of *Antrim* and *Plymouth* along with the RFA *Tidespring*.

By the 18th April all the major Royal Navy assets were at Ascension Island undergoing the vital task of cross decking supplies and equipment. This was completed by the 18th April when the Task Force set sail from Ascension to be on station around the Falklands by the 1st May. The full task force was assembled off the islands by the 24th April and was ready to be deployed. The first task of the fleet was to enforce a Total Exclusion Zone around the islands and begin to draw out the Argentine Navy and Air Force and bring them to battle. This was a vital part of the operation as a landing could not very well take place unless the air and naval threats were at least significantly diminished.

South Georgia was recaptured on the 26th April after a heart stopping night of tension involving the SAS in an abortive landing on the island. The Royal Navy helicopters landed the SAS on the Fortuna Glacier but had to then withdraw them due to severe weather. This was done luckily without casualties, however it left the small task force with a problem in that how can they re-take South Georgia. The senior Royal Marine officer present decided to gather up as many men as possible from the Marines, SAS and SBS and drive ashore under the covering fire of the warships. This tactic worked and the island was re-taken without loss. In the process an Argentine submarine, *Santa Fe* was crippled in Grytvicken harbour by Royal Navy helicopters. The news of this delightful operation was passed back to the government with the immortal words *'Be pleased to inform Her Majesty that the Union Jack flies alongside the White Ensign on South Georgia. God save the Queen'*. Three days later this small force rejoined the main Task Force and on the 30th April the Task Force proceeded inside the Total Exclusion Zone.

Now began the operation to put the islands under pressure and draw out the Argentine Air Force and Navy. On 1st May Port Stanley airfield was bombed in a daring operation showing great navigational skill and endurance by Vulcan bombers of the RAF flying out of Ascension. The raid was followed by an attack by sea harriers and gunfire from *Glamorgan*, *Arrow* and *Alacrity*. The response from the Argentine Air Force was soon to come with a strike on the bombardment group which was beaten off by sea harriers who shot down three aircraft without loss. There was minor damage to *Arrow*. This fairly small engagement had vital consequences in that the Argentine aircraft would never again take on the sea harriers in air-to-air combat. In future their tactics would employ small groups slipping through the defences to attack ships. Another attack was carried out on an Argentine submarine the *San Luis* by helicopters and the submarine was forced to withdraw.

The attention of the Task Force now turned to the Argentine surface fleet. This was a formidable, albeit small fleet, consisting of a carrier, a cruiser and six destroyers (two of them Type 42s). Two of the destroyers (US Gearing Class) were definitely armed with Exocet missiles and the cruiser, *General Belgrano*, was suspected of being armed with Exocet. The Argentine Navy had split into two groups, one made up of the *Belgrano* and the two Exocet armed destroyers and the other of the carrier, *Veinticinco De Mayo* and escorting destroyers. Woodward feared an impending pincer attack and asked for permission to remove one of the pincers. This was a controversial request as the two groups were out of the designated TEZ. However legally any attack could be justified by the warning given by the UK Government through the UN that any hostile shipping deemed to be a threat to the Task Force could be attacked even if outside of the TEZ. The naval staff agreed with Woodward and ordered the SSKs to close with the groups and engage. The SSK hunting the carrier group could not locate the enemy ships but the nuclear-powered hunter killer, *Conqueror* spotted and began tracking the *Belgrano* group.

A request to attack was sent to the naval staff by *Conqueror* and permission given by the Prime Minister and the War Cabinet to do so. A controversial act certainly but militarily a necessary one. One must always remember that had one of the carriers been sunk or badly damaged the operation would have been over for the Task Force. Some MPs and commentators have called this sinking a criminal act but they fail to realise that at some time in a war it is inevitable that military necessity must take over from political considerations and this was one such time. The controversy was essentially that the *Belgrano* was outside the TEZ and steering away from the Falklands. The Admiralty and British Government however were concerned that she could immediately turn north and head for the task force, a manoeuvre that could be carried out in less than a minute. Such a manoeuvre would take her over the Birdwood Bank, a shallow area where *Conqueror* would not be able to follow and contact would most certainly have been lost so the order was given to attack her and the *Belgrano* was sunk with huge loss of life. It was expected that the escorting destroyers would rescue survivors but this was not the case. The destroyers and the carrier group fled for home and shallow waters never to intervene again. Thus, the naval part of the enemy was neutralized at the expense of three torpedoes from the last war. Information made available after the war showed that the Argentine Government had indeed given orders on 1st May, for the pincer attack to go ahead, however the orders were withdrawn when it became clear that the British were not landing on the islands. The threat still remained however and the action can in my opinion be justified. Belgrano was not on peace time manoeuvres and constituted a serious threat to the task force. Sadly, the loss of life was large and it meant that a peaceful resolution to the crisis was not now possible, although this was not likely anyway. It also removed the threat of the *Belgrano* intervening in the later landings which were clearly her orders and who knows what effect she might have had in that action. Had she got close enough her guns could have wreaked havoc on the British shipping in the confined waters of San Carlos.

The Argentine response was swift and deadly when on 4th May, Argentine Super Etendards launched two Exocet missiles at the Type 42 destroyers, *Sheffield* and *Glasgow* who were on the outer ring of defence. One Exocet was decoyed by *Glasgow's* chaff but the second hit *Sheffield* amid ships. The missile failed to explode but the fuel ignited causing a devastating fire which gutted the brand-new destroyer. *Sheffield* was abandoned and foundered on the 10th May. The 4th May also saw the loss of a sea harrier shot down over Goose Green.

The Fleet withdrew slightly to the east to give Woodward time to reorganize his resources and plug the gap left by the *Sheffield*. On 6th May however, more misfortune dogged Woodward when two sea Harriers collided with each other and were lost. On the night of the 9th May Woodward tried his new tactic of a combination of a Type 42 destroyer, *Coventry* and a Type 22 frigate, *Broadsword* to lay off Port Stanley and shoot down aircraft attempting to land and take off from Stanley airfield. These 'combos' as they came to be known were highly successful and were a perfect combination with each ship complementing the other. Their two different air defence systems were linked electronically and between them they were able to guide sea harriers into an attack on the Argentine surveillance ship *Narwhal* which was later sunk. The Combo took up station and Sea Dart was used to attack a Hercules transport which was forced to turn back. Later a Puma helicopter was shot down, the first kill for the Sea Dart system.

Thoughts of course had been placed on where to set ashore the land element. It was clear that the air war could not be won in time to allow an uncontested landing by the Argentine Air Force. It was hoped that the choice of the landing area along with the destroyer and frigate combos could defend the landing close in whilst the sea harriers intercepted further out. In any event a landing would have to take place soon as the months were drawing on and the weather getting steadily worse. San Carlos Water was chosen as the landing site for the invasion. It was further from Port Stanley than the military would have liked but the anchorage was covered by low lying hills which would hinder air attack. In any event there were large Chinook helicopters on the way from Ascension which could lift the land element forward. On the 10/11th May *Alacrity* was sent into San Carlos Water to check for mines, finding the water clear she proceeded to sink an Argentine transport with gunfire before returning to rejoin the fleet.

The plan of drawing out the Argentine Air Force continued a pace, and on the 12th May the task force was attacked by eight Skyhawks. At first the combo of *Glasgow* and *Brilliant* had trouble with the low flying fast attackers due to the salt encrusted missile launchers on the Sea Dart system. However, the Sea Wolf of *Brilliant* performed magnificently and brought down three of the attackers. The remaining four Skyhawks were more successful as yet again Sea Dart failed and Sea Wolf also failed to function reducing the combo to old-fashioned machine-gun fire. *Glasgow* was hit but the bomb was dropped too low and failed to detonate, a common occurrence during the war. Argentine pilots were highly skilled and very courageous but their ordnance let them down many times, mainly because the bombs were dropped too low and failed to arm.

As the landing forces approached the island *Glamorgan* assisted an SAS raid on Pebble Island with naval gunfire. This highly successful raid destroyed eleven Pucara aircraft and left the way open for a landing. On the 17th May *Invincible* left the fleet briefly to fly off SAS personnel who landed in southern Argentina to report on aircraft taking off. The landing on East Falkland took place on the night of the 20th May guarded by the fleet. The carrier task group remained out at sea whilst seven ships were sent in to San Carlos Water to provide point defence for the landings and the transports. The Argentine response to the landings was not long in coming. Daggers and Macchi 339 aircraft attacked on the 21st May causing damage to *Argonaut*. One dagger was shot down by a Sea Cat from *Plymouth* but the *Antrim* was hit by a bomb that again failed to explode. A second wave of Daggers hit *Antrim* again with cannon fire but one was shot down by Sea Wolf from *Broadsword*.

HMS *Ardent* was bombarding Goose Green airfield at this time in order to prevent Pucaras from taking off. One was destroyed on the ground by *Ardent's* gunfire and the rest successfully driven off by her machine guns, one being shot down by a Sea Harrier. *Ardent* was then attacked by four Skyhawks, two of which were shot down by Sea Harriers. Skyhawks then attacked *Argonaut* hitting her with two bombs which failed to explode. This raid was followed by four Daggers, one of which was shot down by a Sea Harrier. These

Daggers went for *Broadsword* and *Brilliant* causing minor damage. HMS *Ardent* was then the target of more Daggers and Skyhawks which scored nine bomb hits, all but two of which exploded. Three of these attackers were shot down by Sea Harriers but *Ardent* was in a bad way and had to be abandoned.

This had been a hard day's continuous fighting but had resulted in ten Argentine aircraft being shot down by Sea Harriers alone. But Woodward was very concerned as the attrition on his ships was serious. Two key points should be noted here though.

1. The Argentines had concentrated their attacks on the warships not the transports and landing craft allowing the landing to continue unhindered.
2. The Argentine Air Force had been forced to drop their bombs at too low level and as mentioned before they constantly failed to explode.

The fighting on the 23rd was very similar in scale and ferocity to the 22nd. The Task Force group was reinforced by another Type 42 destroyer, *Exeter*, along with two more frigates *Ambuscade* and the ill-fated *Antelope*. *Antelope* was ordered closer inshore within San Carlos Water to protect the amphibious assault ships but was hit by a bomb dropped from a Skyhawk which failed to explode on impact. However, during attempts later that night to diffuse the bomb it exploded sending the newly arrived frigate to the bottom. The Argentines lost two aircraft, one to the Royal Navy ships and one to a Sea Harrier. Air attacks resumed again on the 24th and the Argentines lost three Daggers to Sea Harriers and the Royal Navy ships accounted for another Skyhawk. However, two landing ships were hit by bombs which failed to explode.

The 25th was rather a black day for the Royal Navy. The *Coventry/ Broadsword* combo was placed to the north in order to intercept aircraft as they flew in to begin their runs. Having shot down two Skyhawks early in the morning the ships were singled out for repeated attacks by Argentine aircraft. Four Skyhawks made an attack run on *Broadsword* whose Sea Wolf malfunctioned and a bomb hit, again failing to explode. *Coventry* was then attacked and due to the fact that she thought she had a firing solution on the attacking aircraft she called off the Sea Harriers that were coming to her aid. *Coventry* was hit by three bombs and sank almost straight away. Further out to sea a Super Etendard was skimming the ocean looking for a target and launched her Exocet at one of the carriers. The missile lost track and then acquired another target, the freighter *Atlantic Conveyor*. The freighter sank taking the expected and very valuable Chinook helicopters with her and thus forcing the land elements to walk to Port Stanley.

The 25th was the last major assault on the Task Force ships and the most successful day for the Argentines. The land element was now well ashore and beginning its march on Port Stanley fighting as they went. The Task Force was reinforced by two more destroyers and several frigates and continued to provide support for the land campaign. One last attack was carried out on the frigate, *Avenger* who was caught alone returning from dropping SAS troops on a clandestine mission. The last Argentine Exocet was fired on *Avenger* but she decoyed it with chaff. The Royal Navy ships finally assisted with the assault on Port Stanley by providing gunfire support but having beaten off the Argentine Navy and Air Force the Task Force had completed its mission with flying colours.

I think it only right now to commend the bravery and skill of the Argentine pilots. They were flying aircraft not really designed for this kind of action at very low level. Their bravery in the execution of their missions was quite astonishing and the Task Force was greatly impressed. Had the Argentine surface fleet and above all the army fought with such skill and bravery then things may have turned out quite different in the war.

Indeed, one could quite easily throw a huge number of 'ifs' into this conflict. If more bombs had exploded, if the Argentines had acquired more Exocet from France (and it was certainly the case that they were trying, but a joint approach by both MI6 and the French

Government was instrumental in preventing this). If the Exocet had acquired one of the carriers as its target and not *Atlantic Conveyor*, if the Argentine Navy had pressed its attack even after losing the *Belgrano* the carrier and the Exocet armed destroyers could have sunk a Royal Navy carrier. If the air attacks had concentrated on the landing and supply ships and not the warships. The ifs can of course go on forever but there is no doubt that the Argentines made serious errors in judgment and strategy in what should perhaps have been an easy to win confrontation. But as we see throughout history success often favours the bold and for Britain to send a fleet eight thousand miles south into hostile waters and into the striking range of an effective air force, one cannot get bolder.

The ramifications of this great British victory are still being felt to this day. Politically it gave the Conservative party and its leader Mrs Thatcher a suit of political armour which would not be broken for fifteen years. Without victory in the Falklands there would have been no 'Thatcherism' and no major economic changes. It sent a clear message to the world that dictators and bullying nations will be curbed wherever they are, so long as Britain has reach. A doctrine that Britain was able to share with her key Allies especially the United States as we later see with armed interventions in the former Yugoslavia and Balkans and of course against Iraq in two subsequent wars. Mrs Thatcher in her memoirs *The Downing Street Years* states that in conversations with acquaintances in the Soviet Union that the Soviet Government and military did not think we would fight and if we did, we would lose. This one war sent a huge message internationally to would be enemies and dictators. It was also of course a godsend to the Royal Navy as the cutbacks would stop and no British Government whatever their colour would consider withdrawing the naval presence from the rest of the world. It has also led to the aircraft carrier reasserting itself as the primary conventional warship of the Royal Navy with the building of the new class of super carriers *Queen Elizabeth* and *Prince of Wales.*

Epilogue

With two thirds of the world covered in water it is inevitable that war at sea will take place and the campaigns we have studied in this book highlight how naval engagements can change world history. They can make and break empires, stop ambitious conquest and assert authority and dominance over vast areas. They lead the way in technological development and achievement and push forward industrial change and expansion as well as economic growth. In the 21st century we see navies strengthened by man's achievements in space with the advent of modern satellites and communications allowing ships to control vast areas of the oceans and strike far in land with missiles launched from ships and submarines at sea. Strength at sea is still a recognised form of promoting influence and prestige, nothing gives a more powerful signal than a warship coming into a foreign port or carrying out manoeuvres in areas that are in the world's eye. In particular I think of the vast US fleets constantly on station in areas such as the South China Sea and Indian Ocean. The former is a crucial deployment and has without doubt stopped China's ambitions to invade Taiwan. Closer to home we see NATO ships operating in the Black Sea deterring an ever more aggressive Russia and reminding Putin that NATO's reach is long and with ships like the Royal Navy's Type 45 destroyers deadly, thus giving, one hopes, pause for thought.

But above all they show man at his most ingenious providing a stage for his endeavours that has been captured in poetry and art, even on the walls of our palaces of government making heroes out of successful leaders and giving mythological status to ships and events.